REGULAR ARMIES AND INSURGENCY

REGULAR ARMIES
AND INSURGENCY

EDITED BY RONALD HAYCOCK

CROOM HELM LONDON
ROWMAN AND LITTLEFIELD TOTOWA N.J.

© 1979 Ronald Haycock
Croom Helm Ltd, 2–10 St John's Road, London SW11

British Library Cataloguing in Publication Data

Military History Symposium, *5th*
   Royal Military College of Canada, 1978
   Regular armies and insurgency.
   1. Revolutions – History – 20th century
   – Congresses
   2. Armed Forces – History – 20th century
   – Congresses
   I. Title II. Haycock, Ronald
   III. Royal Military College of Canada
   909.82   D431

   ISBN 0-85664-787-X

First published in the United States 1979 by
Rowman and Littlefield
81 Adams Drive
Totowa, New Jersey

ISBN 0-8476-6200-4

Jacket photograph, courtesy of John McClancy

Printed in Great Britain by
Biddles Ltd, Guildford, Surrey

CONTENTS

PREFACE AND ACKNOWLEDGEMENTS

The papers comprising this volume were first read before the Fifth
Annual Military History Symposium held at the Royal Military College
of Canada on 30 and 31 March 1978. The theme of the conference
was particularly topical. On almost a daily basis we are bombarded by
the news media with reports of clashes between regular armies and
insurgents. Iran, Rhodesia, Angola, Northern Ireland and Ethiopia are
but a few of the places mentioned. Whether layman, scholar or soldier,
one cannot help but be concerned with these disturbing events, or
indeed remember the vivid days of the collapse of South Vietnam
without some serious reflection.

Certainly since the Second World War there has been no lack of
individual accounts, both learned and journalistic, of specific
insurgencies, and for some time now scholars have been increasingly
aware of the varied aspects of insurgent and counter-insurgent warfare.
With these considerations in mind then, we at RMC decided to bring
together for a symposium some of the more renowned experts to
discuss five representative situations involving regular armies and
insurgency in the twentieth century.

For the purposes of the conference and subsequently of this
volume, the first presentation was meant to provide a general commen-
tary on the theme, and to act as an introduction to the other five
essays. Clearly our objectives were to bring before a concerned audience
a group of leading scholars and to present historical examples of the
theme. But more than this, we aimed to show the similarities and
differences in each situation, and to explore the effects of various
factors such as politics, culture, and economics as well as military
considerations for regular armies when dealing with insurgency.

As in the past we owe a great deal to the Department of National
Defence and to the Canada Council, for without their financial support
the symposium would never have occurred. It is also a pleasure to thank
RMC's Commandant, Brigadier-General A.J.G.D. de Chastelain, for his
enthusiastic interest and support. To his officers and the College Staff
we are especially indebted for their cheerful administrative help in
what was at times an awesome organisational task. Lieutenant-Colonel
Frank Hlohovsky, Director of Administration; Captain Gord Johnson,
Administrative Officer; Sergeant McLean and Mr Fawkes of the Senior

Staff Mess; Mrs Norleen Hope in the Transportation Section; and Mrs Karen Brown of the History Department were particularly helpful in making the Symposium a success. Finally, to those who came to give and those who came to hear these papers, and to our publisher David Croom, we also express our appreciation.

Ronald Haycock
The Royal Military College of Canada
Kingston, Ontario

REGULAR ARMIES AND INSURGENCY

1 REGULAR ARMIES AND INSURGENCY

Sir Robert G.K. Thompson

Conflicts between regular armies and various groups of insurgents, fighting for a range of causes, have affected many parts of the world in recent years: Cyprus, Malaya, Algeria, Latin America, Vietnam, Ulster, Rhodesia and dozens of others. The only thing that they really have in common is that they are all part of what is tantamount to a Third World War, made up of over thirty years of insurgencies, and of far-reaching significance to peoples all over the globe.[1]

This paper deals with regular armies in an insurgency. Irrespective of whether one wishes to refer to insurgency, rebellion or whatever, the general situation which exists in these cases is that the regular army must deal with an armed uprising which has the intention of overthrowing the government of its country and changing, in most cases, the country's complete political and social systems. The insurgency may be supported from outside the country, and in this case there are differences between infiltration, raids and invasion. Infiltration is where supplies and manpower, and particularly trained and specialist manpower, come in from across the border to aid insurgency. A raid exists when units from outside make an incursion into the country for limited objectives and then go out again. At this point lines blur somewhat, for it is possible for a raiding unit with, say, ten days' supplies for a single objective, to expand its operations if the opportunities present themselves during the raid to secure further supplies and exploit more targets. However, generally speaking, infiltration and raids are the two forms of outside support in an insurgency. The third aspect, direct invasion, is not complementary to insurgency but is a substitute for it. Such a case, of course, existed after 1972 in Vietnam because the insurgency failed and it was replaced by straight invasion from the outside.

One of the very difficult things for a regular army to understand, is that an undefeated army can lose a war. It is the cardinal aim of an insurgent movement, by using guerrilla techniques, tactics and strategy, to render a superior army incapable of saving the state. The basic winning formula for an insurgency is as follows: if an insurgent movement can, at a cost which is indefinitely acceptable, impose costs on a government which are not indefinitely acceptable, then, while losing every battle, it is winning the war. In short, the army wins all the battles and is still defeated in the end. However, costs on both sides are not comparable. Quite obviously in a democracy great problems arise with the occurrence of heavy casualties and heavy taxation – not the least of which is the problem of political support. In a totalitarian regime or one which acts under the strong discipline of a communist movement, the citizen may not even know what the costs are. Furthermore, even if the casualties and the taxes are heavy, these factors do not have the same political cost. There is no question of the government being turned out. To demonstrate this, during the Vietnam war an American Congressman said to me in 1966 that he could stand only so many casualties and only so many tax increases then he would lose his bid for re-election. Clearly then this is where the costs are liable to differ between both sides in an insurgency.

Fifteen years ago, in my book *Defeating Communist Insurgency*, I laid down five principles covering the 'dos' and 'don'ts' in such conflicts.[2] The first one is that there must be a very clear political aim – that is you must know what political end you seek. In many cases, for example in Vietnam, few people really knew what they meant by winning the war. Unless it is clear in your mind what you are trying to do and what you mean by winning, then you simply cannot assess what your actions and operations are doing because the key thing is that all actions and all operations must contribute to the political aim. If they do not, then they are at best wasted and at worst counter-productive.

The second point about counter-insurgency is that the whole government side, the army, police and civil administration, must function in accordance with the law of the land, and in accordance with the highest civilised standards. This cannot be stressed strongly enough. It means that normal procedures of justice must continue; excellent discipline and good control must be maintained; and errors should be admitted – for they will occur. During the Vietnam conflict a massacre such as My Lai was always likely in the circumstances existing at the time. It is to be hoped that nothing quite on that scale will happen, but those on the government side, especially those in the regular armies, must expect that things will go wrong at some point. When that happens the error must be admitted, and admitted quickly and clearly, because there are a number of practical things at stake here: what the government stands for, its credibility, the whole prospect of reconciliation at the end. Coming back to the political aim, this must be a polity which is reconciled again as far as can be achieved. In this regard such considerations as the term of surrender policy for the insurgents are vital to establishing a reconciled and hence stable country. All this depends on what the government stands for during the insurgency. For instance, it is very important that a defecting rebel must trust his former enemies and continue to do so when he comes over to the government side. This principle is perhaps the most important consideration when regular armies deal with insurgency.

The third point is that there must be an overall plan and an overall strategy. An insurgency covers every single field of government and politics and of the military and society. There is no such thing as 'the other war', a term which was used a lot in Vietnam. There is only one all-encompassing conflict and regular armies are part of every aspect of it.

The key thing in any counter-insurgency is organisation.[3] The government side and its forces are up against an efficient organisation and must therefore be just as efficient themselves. Clearly part of being organised is the psychological benefit for regular armies of coping with insurgency. Counter-insurgents must show that they are as efficient and capable as the other side. This particularly applies in the intelligence field where organisation is paramount. Intelligence can be too easily neglected, especially by the over-enthusiastic, such as one American General in Vietnam who said: 'Oh let's go out and kill some Viet Cong and then we can worry about intelligence'. Unfortunately, this is typical of generals.

Another important yet unemphasised consideration for regular armies in an insurgency is the public relations and the psychological warfare side.[4] The latter is important not only for its use against the enemy but for gaining the support of the country at large. Insufficient attention in regular armies is paid to this area and, all too often, the public relations officer of military headquarters, the man who talks to the press, is a passed-over lieutenant-colonel. Information is one of the major instruments of war, and a great deal of care must be exercised in its use. Consequently, information officers must be very high grade officers. They must know exactly what is going on, and the commander himself must also act as his own information officer on occasions. Indeed, it is vital that he should do so. One additional point about organisation — the creation of a vast regular army should be avoided. A vast regular army throws the whole country right out of balance, especially politically. In most societies it is very hard to disband a large regular army. Another important consideration — and this is observable in many countries — is that a regular soldier costs twice as much as a policeman or anyone else like him. The soldier is the most expensive of the weapons which the government has available. Therefore it does not want too many of them because — returning to the cost formula mentioned earlier — one of the aims of the overall plan and strategy is economy of effort.

The last two principles are, from the military point of view, by far the most important. They are the most specific concern of the army and they go very much together. The first of these two is: secure your own base areas. By base areas is meant not just cities, ports, airfields, roads and so on, but the developed, cultivated, populated areas of the countryside. These are going to be the key to the war. They must be secured, and firmly, on the government side. Secondly, the priority of attack should be against the insurgents' infrastructure, not against their guerrilla units. The word priority is used here in its strict meaning. If the enemy are already coming through the windows — and it may be the major effect if you have reached the 'window' stage — they must, of course, be kept out of the windows. But the priority still remains to break their infrastructure.[5]

To put the last two principles in other terms, the government's aims must be to secure its own assets and to deny those assets to the other side. Obviously these are very sensible strategic goals. However, care must be exercised, for in seeking such aims a government is increasing its military commitments. The one thing that can go completely wrong when a government tries to increase its security is that it only increases its military commitment by areas. If it reaches such a position it will suddenly find out that such over-expansion has completely destroyed its security. In short, it must make sure that increasing its own safety by areas does not overcommit the forces that are available. To elaborate on this last point: the major temptation for any army when incidents occur in an insurgency, and most incidents will occur somewhere out in the remote villages and areas, is to stampede out with everything it has got into those areas. This is the normal type of 'search and destroy' attitude. The whole point of these sorts of incidents is to get the army thoroughly committed to areas of minor concern with the result that it gets tied down there. This course leaves the base areas, that is to say, the developed, populated areas of the countryside, open to penetration until, suddenly, the army finds it has lost them. As soon as this starts to happen the immediate threat then is to the towns and cities, and the situation is rapidly reached where the army is hauled back just to defend the urban areas. Once put in this posture the regular army finds itself turned into a static garrison completely undefeated but with the whole place just about to collapse.

The answer to this problem is to have some well-trained, elite units to strike at the guerrillas out in the remote areas in a long-range penetration role. This is not the same as what was referred to in Vietnam as 'picnic lunch' operations where troops were ferried in by helicopter in the morning, brought lunch at one o'clock and then were helicoptered out again at five. If troops are going to fight in these areas, they must go in and stay, regardless of how they get there. Once in position the regular troops must fight like the enemy. In other words, one must really operate just like the guerrillas in those areas. This tactic aims to keep the enemy occupied by the use of the regular army's elite long-range penetration units while the bulk of the forces establish a security framework in their own base areas.

In many cases of insurgency warfare, the concept of strategic hamlets is very important for regular forces.[6] The British used it in the Malayan Emergency, and the Americans tried to apply it in Vietnam. Unfortunately, the latter, prior to 1969, were doing exactly what they should not do in such a vital programme where the consequences can be so costly. In brief, the regular forces tried to deal first with the worst rebel-infected area, where they would choose, say, three villages and attempt to turn these into strategic hamlets, only to suddenly realise that they needed a battalion each to be held. The fundamental error of such a decision was that security declined and commitments increased drastically. The answer is to start at the easier points and work outwards. The reason for this is that regular forces should be trying to achieve a situation where the less contested areas can be held by the local people so that the army is free all the time to go on fighting insurgents in more vital areas. Although the British did not get it anywhere near right or anywhere near perfect, this is roughly what was done in Malaya and, rather surprisingly, what was almost repeated, successfully, in Vietnam between 1969 and 1971.

In 1968, just after the Tet Offensive and the implementation of the 'search and destroy' policy, Henry Kissinger was advised that US strategy in Vietnam was misdirected to the extent that a policy of 'clear and hold' was far more efficient than one of 'search and destroy'. After hearing the rationale, the details of which have already been explained in this essay, Kissinger was also told that if such a course was adopted, within one year one hundred thousand US troops could be withdrawn without jeopardising the situation. As events turned out, in 1971 after such a 'clear and hold' scheme had been in effect, all but about 50,000 Americans had departed Vietnam without causing the situation there to collapse. It is quite clear that a regular force, by securing its own bases, can indirectly impede the infrastructure of an insurgency. However, that infrastructure must be attacked directly. If a guerrilla unit is going to operate it has to have easy sources of supply, food, ammunition, information and recruits, and some organisation has to provide these just like a government provides them for its own forces. It is this organisation that has to be broken. Now, in most military thinking the normal process which regular armies are supposed to go through is to defeat the enemy's main forces in the field, to disrupt their rear bases and to break their will to resist or attack, as the case may be. Even though regular armies must fight the enemy's main combat units at some time, this should not be their principal objective. What must be done is to disrupt the enemy's rear bases and to break his entire operating system. Few American military men realised this point during the Vietnam war, until General Abrams, one of the most able generals of his generation, came on the scene. He understood completely the necessity of breaking the insurgency's infrastructure. During Abrams' tenure, it was quite fascinating to hear his subordinate generals in Vietnam, who had previously espoused the faulty 'body-count' strategy before Abrams arrived there, to be now saying that their job was to break the enemy's system. One of them even proudly proclaimed to me on one visit that he had 'got 300 bicycles yesterday'. This time he had the strategy correct. Those 300 bicycles were a very important supply element to the other side. They were the whole means of movement of supplies to a large section of their forces, and the destruction of them was far more important to the entire movement than a few counted dead bodies would have been.

One further point about the enemy's infrastructure must be made and that is that his freedom of movement must be denied. In the course of any insurgency, hundreds if not thousands of people are keeping the rebel movement going by carrying supplies, delivering messages, sending recruits and many other necessities. This mobility takes place both in the urban as well as the hinterland areas. It must be seriously curtailed if not stopped altogether. However, the regular force must never exhaust its entire effectiveness in a massive control programme. For instance, pressure can be taken off regular army units by consigning police units to clamp down on the insurgents' freedom of movement near the urban areas, while elite units of the regular force penetrate the hinterland. The latter case does not call for large patrolling forces, but for long-range penetration units who are prepared to go in there and stay for three or four weeks, as quite small parties, sitting on trails, setting up ambushes and generally harassing the insurgents' movements. The principal result for the enemy is that his system breaks down as his mobility becomes more difficult. Perhaps one should look back to World War II and the days of the Battle of the Atlantic. The German submarines attempted to deny our mobility and hence crack our infrastructure. There was a similar situation in Burma. When the British were finally conquering that country and were on the way down to Rangoon, there was a two-corps front, two main prongs with two divisions in each corps but with regiments of tanks and artillery and everything else, pushing down Burma. There were enormous quantities of trucks and other equipment. The basic necessities were food, petrol and ammunition in large quantities. Since there was no real road into this theatre of operations the only feasible way to bring in the vital supplies was by air. In the dry season there was no problem in the flights or the comparatively simple task of constructing temporary air strips for the C-47s. The serious problems, however, stemmed from the numbers of aircraft necessary to keep four divisions operating. It was found that it did not require that many if the aircraft were kept 'streaming'. In other words, they would take off from their bases in Assam, come into their allotted airfield, drop their loads, go straight back, fill up, and come in again. They could do five trips in daylight if they were streaming. Now this was the key, the absolute key, to the whole of the operations. The Japanese had seven Zeros, a small but formidable air force if they had been used properly. Fortunately they were not. Often they came in and shot up the leading trucks going down the road, a tactic which only delayed the advance for very short periods. If the enemy aircraft had got into the streams of the Dakotas, and if transport command had then demanded fighter escorts, the ground columns would have been seriously impeded in their progress if not stopped altogether. Because the British would have had to escort the Dakotas in convoys, and because they would not have got more than two trips a day out of them, they could not have advanced on the ground when being supplied by that limited number of aircraft. The general point illustrated by these examples is that in denying freedom of movement, one must find the enemy's weak spots, and when these are attacked his entire infrastructure crumbles. One final point to be made about the strategic importance of attacking an insurgency's infrastructure is that it makes it very difficult for the enemy to infiltrate the government side when its own system is under heavy pressure. Similarly, attacks on the enemy's organisation make it less able to build up guerrilla force units.

Concentrating intelligence on the enemy's infrastructure, then, must always be a major strategic concern for any regular force. To ignore this aspect of counter-insurgency warfare is to court disaster.[7]

A point beyond the five principles already discussed is the one of strategic initiative. The Americans always thought they had it in Vietnam because they could get into a helicopter and go anywhere they liked. That is not strategic initiative. Going back to World War II, the Allies did not have strategic initiative until about 1943, when the requirements for strategic initiative, a secure base and a secure line of communication to the front, were gained. If bases are absolutely secure — in 1943 the United States bases were unchallenged and even in the British Isles the invasion and bomber threats were all but over — and if lines of communications to the front are secure, then strategic initative is won, as it was by late 1943 with the Allies. The moment this position is reached, then one can decide the moment of attack, its point of concentration and how much force to use.

So far the discussion has centred on insurgency with its bases inside the threatened country but there are many examples where guerrilla centres exist outside the contested territory. In this connection infiltration and raids have been mentioned. If regular forces are to have strategic initiative they must render the enemy's main rear bases insecure, and in some cases, the regular armies must be prepared to cross borders to do it. The British certainly did this in Borneo. Admittedly these border infractions were kept very quiet. Gurkha troops were used, fighting at night and with kukris so that there was a maximum amount of terror for the enemy and as little as possible telltale expenditure of ammunition. Such raids also help spoil future action by insurgents. It is not at all surprising that Rhodesia, for example, has made such long sorties into rebel-infested neighbouring territory in the particular circumstances. Without commenting otherwise on this conflict it is a perfectly natural counter-move for Rhodesia to spoil the operations that the other side are mounting across the borders by putting her own forces into their territory.

In any insurgency, of course, if people are coming from outside and if this is publicly and actively supported by neighbouring governments then one need not be — all other things being equal — denied the use of bombing.[8] However, one should differentiate between the American bombing operations of 1965 and 1968 in Indo-China and those of 1972, by which point the Americans had many marvellous guided weapons, the laser bomb among others. There is little similarity between those two periods. An air force now is a very surgical instrument in cross-border operations.

One of the best examples of cross-border raids was the American penetration of Cambodia in 1970. It seems that toward the end of the operation, Kissinger, then the President's advisor on National Security, was in a quandary about how much time the raid would gain for the American forces before Hanoi could mount a major offensive against the south. On one hand most of his intelligence officers cynically suggested only a three month respite; on the other, one special advisor pointed out — correctly so as it turned out — that at least a year, probably eighteen months and just possibly two years had been gained. The latter opinion was based on the raid's effect of closing the major port of entry (Sihanoukville) to Russian and Chinese ships which were directly supplying the Communists' war machine in the south — a point which Kissinger's intelligence officers seem to have missed in their apparent single-minded fascination with the amount of warstuffs destroyed or captured in the Cambodian raid. Clearly, with the major sea port closed the insurgent forces in South Vietnam would be dependent directly on Hanoi for their supplies through the long Ho Chi Minh Trail. This passage could not be extended and enlarged in less than twelve months at a minimum by the North Vietnamese. This episode demonstrates quite clearly that when assessing intelligence information one must consider quite carefully the widest possible effects rather than simply those gained as a result of captured and destroyed equipment and personnel.

One further point which was a key element in the Vietnam war and one which people do not realise was probably its turning point, was the Laos Agreement of 1962.[9] Because it kept the United States out of Laos and gave the North Vietnamese a free run it made the war almost unwinnable. The effect of this treaty on the Laotian government was far less important than the effect it had on the war in Vietnam, for the North Vietnamese paid no attention at all to the agreement. What mattered in that accord was one little line — no foreign troops in Laos. That is what the Communists wanted in it and that is what Mr Averill Harriman gave them. And as a result of that we had the 'Averill Harriman Freeway'. As soon as such a document was signed, the Americans lost an important aspect of their freedom of choice, knowing full well that they would keep their part of the agreement or try to if the Senate Foreign Relations Committee had anything to do with it. Who on the North Vietnamese side would see that the bargain was kept — an International Control Commission with Poles or Hungarians or whatever on it? The other side knew perfectly well that

they would then have a free run down through Laos. If they had not
had this unmolested avenue through Laos, the insurgency in Vietnam
could have been stopped at any time in the early 1960s. In this regard
it should also be noted that as a strategic stroke, if any American
forces were going to be used, the correct place to put them was in the
northern part of the panhandle of Southern Laos, where there were
few people and where the US forces could stop the whole thing there
and then. What is more, the other side would have had to come and
fight them on ground very much to the advantage of the United States.[10]
Therefore, any regular army must have someone with the capability of
advising properly these amateur politicians and diplomats when they
are conducting negotiations with the other side.

Unsound diplomacy is only a specific mistake of countering insurgents. There can be more fundamental errors. In any endeavour
involving organised conflict there are three elements — policy, strategy
and tactics. One can look back to Vietnam in 1968 when the leaders
there wanted an additional 200,000 men. This was strategy dictating
policy. By the same token, tactics must support the strategy. It could
be argued that in part the war in Vietnam was lost by helicopters
because soldiers would not get on their feet. In other words, a regular
army should be careful to make sure that the seemingly miraculous
innovations in tactical military technology do not lead it strategically
astray. For regular forces fighting insurgents there are no gimmicks or
shortcuts to success.

Very clear strategic thinking is absolutely essential; and this requires
good intelligence and accurate reporting. When an intelligence officer
brings bad news he should be promoted, for he is an honest man. If one
is not very careful, intelligence may be tailored to fit policy: this is one
of the reasons we are losing World War III.

Notes

1. Robert Thompson, *Revolutionary War in World Strategy 1945–1969*
(Secker and Warburg, London, 1970). In this work, the author discusses various
aspects of twenty-five years of those global insurgencies, particularly as promoted
and supported by Russian and Chinese foreign policy.

2. See Chapter 4 in the author's *Defeating Communist Insurgency:
Experiences from Malaya and Vietnam* (Chatto and Windus, London, 1966).

3. Thompson, *Revolutionary War*, pp. 5 and 123–4.

4. Thompson, *Defeating Communist Insurgency*, Chapter 8.

5. Ibid., pp. 55–8.

6. For an elaboration of the concept of strategic hamlets, see ibid., Chapter
II, pp. 121–40.

7. Destruction of the enemy's infrastructure and the relevant experiences in Burma during 1945 are discussed by Sir Robert Thompson in his *No Exit From Vietnam* (Chatto and Windus, London, 1969).
8. Ibid., pp. 93–7.
9. Thompson, *Revolutionary War*, pp. 127–8.
10. Thompson, *No Exit from Vietnam*, pp. 31, 43–4 and 69–70.

Further Reading

Castro, Fidel, *Revolutionary Struggle, 1947–1958*, R.E. Binahcea and N.P. Valdés (eds.) (Massachusetts Institute of Technology Press, Cambridge, 1972)

Clutterbuck, Richard, *Living with Terrorism* (Faber, London, 1975)

Debray, Régis, *Revolution in the Revolution?* (MR Press, New York, 1972)

——, *Strategy for Revolution*, Robin Blackburn (ed.) (MR Press, New York, 1970)

Eckstein, Harry (ed.), *Internal War, Problems and Approaches* (Free Press of Glencoe, New York, 1964)

Fairbairn, Geoffrey, *Revolutionary Guerrilla Warfare, the Countryside Version* (Penguin, Baltimore, 1964)

Galula, David, *Counter-insurgency Warfare; Theory and Practice* (Praeger, New York, 1964)

Giap, Vo-Nguyen, *People's War, People's Army* (Praeger, New York, 1962)

Guevara, Ernesto, *Ché Guevara on Guerrilla Warfare* (Praeger, New York, 1961)

Hodges, Donald C. (ed.), *Abraham Guillen: Philosophy of the Urban Guerrilla* (Morrow, New York, 1973)

Johnson, Chalmers, *Autopsy on People's Wars* (University of California Press, Berkeley, 1973)

Laqueur, Walter, *Guerrilla: A Historical and Critical Study* (Little, Brown Brown and Co., Toronto, 1976)

——, *Terrorism* (Weidenfeld and Nicolson, London, 1978)

Tse-Tung, Mao, *On Guerrilla Warfare*, S.B. Griffith (trans.) (Praeger, New York, 1961)

Tse-Tung, Mao, *Selected Works*, vol. 1 (Foreign Languages Press, Peking, 1965)

McCuen, J.J., *The Art of Counter-Revolutionary War* (Faber, London, 1966)

Moss, Robert, *Urban Guerrillas, the New Face of Political Violence*

(Maurice Temple Smith, London, 1972)

Neuberg, A., *Armed Insurrection*, Quintin Homre (trans.) (NLB, London, 1970)

Orlov, Alexander, *Handbook of Intelligence and Guerrilla Warfare* (University of Michigan Press, Ann Arbor, 1963)

Osanka, F.M. (ed.), *Modern Guerrilla Warfare* (Free Press of Glencoe, New York, 1962)

Paget, Julian, *Counter-insurgency Campaigning* (Faber, London, 1967)

Paret, Peter and John Shy, *Guerrillas in the Sixties* (Praeger, New York, 1962)

Pomeroy, William J. (ed.), *Guerrilla Warfare and Marxism* (International Publishers, New York, 1968)

Schreiber, Jan, *The Ultimate Weapon: Terrorists and World Order* (Morrow, New York, 1978)

Taber, Robert, *The War of the Flea: A Study of Guerrilla Warfare, Theory and Practice* (Stuart, New York, 1965)

Thayer, Charles, *Guerrilla* (Joseph, London, 1964)

Wilkinson, Paul, *Terrorism and the Liberal State* (Macmillan, London and Toronto, 1977)

2 REGULAR ARMIES AND INSURGENCY: THE CASE OF MEXICO

Edwin Lieuwen

Basic to our understanding of Mexico's chronic insurgency problem is some appreciation of the unique human and physical geography of that country. Insurgents who campaign successfully against established governments must base their activities in areas between concentrations of population and relatively inaccessible territory. In the populated areas there is something to be done — actual fighting and the enlistment of support, or the seizure of material necessities. Central Mexico, where population and economic activities are concentrated, also has rugged terrain and heavy forest cover, thus providing the ideal juxtaposition of civilisation and wilderness so essential to successful insurgency. It is Mexico's unique geography which largely explains why insurgency was more prevalent there in the nineteenth century than in any country in Latin America.

In the twentieth century, an additional factor became important. The construction, in the late nineteenth century, of three railroad trunk lines from Central Mexico to the distant United States border in the north meant that insurgents could operate successfully in areas remote from population centres. Their source of arms, supplies, and support became the United States, and this was critical in the outcome of all the successful insurgency operations in Mexico since 1910. Mexico's twentieth-century insurgency problem can best be comprehended by viewing it in the context of civil-military relations. What was the issue? Who would run the nation? Would the regular army continue its traditional political monopoly, or would more broadly based civilian forces exercise power? Only a deep social revolution, the world's first in the twentieth century, would decide the outcome. Between 1910 and 1914, the struggle was between the regular army and an armed civilian populace. When the latter ultimately triumphed, it became the revolutionary army. From 1914 to 1920, insurgency was essentially an internecine struggle between factions of the revolutionary army for control of the government. Between 1920 and 1940, the struggle was between the military and civilian (labour-peasant) sectors of the revolutionary coalition. Only after the civilian triumph in 1940 and the subsequent weakening of the regular army did insurgency cease to be a serious problem. Isolated insurgent outbreaks of the past 38 years have come from leftist civilian protests against conservative governments. Since 1940, the regular army has remained completely loyal to the government. It has no longer been a factor in creating insurgency, only in suppressing it.

The outside world was shocked by the sudden overthrow in May 1911 of dictator Porfirio Diaz's government, which had ruled Mexico with little serious opposition for 35 years. General Diaz had demonstrated his political genius in the late nineteenth century by pacifying and disciplining the hitherto intractable regular army. He was the first ruler in Mexican history to bridle the provincial military chieftains and render them subordinate to the central government. Rivals too dangerous to confront in battle he pacified with opportunities for graft and plunder. The loyalty of others he purchased with generous salaries and expense accounts. Many were given the opportunity to forfeit political ambitions in exchange for economic concessions and landed estates. Those who could not be bought were goaded into rebellion, then crushed by superior government forces. To ensure loyalty and to prevent any officer from gaining the personal allegiance of large bodies of enlisted men, he adopted a system of frequent rotation of command posts. Potential rivals were either 'promoted' to governorships or cashiered from the army on charges of corruption.[1]

Diaz's army also began to make the regular army more professional. Observers were sent to St. Cyr and West Point. The latest European training manuals were adopted. Remington rifles were purchased from the United States and artillery pieces from France and Germany. The new Chapultepec Military Academy trained enthusiastic young cadets in the arts of modern warfare. Reputable turn-of-the-century foreign military observers such as Charles Jerram, Thomas Janvier, and Percy Martin were impressed by the growing technical competence, general efficiency, and high morale of Mexico's first truly national army.[2]

And yet, in scarcely 100 days from the beginning of the February 1911 uprisings led by Francisco Madero and Pancho Villa, provincial insurgent bands of peasants, workers, shopkeepers and students, armed with machetes, pistols, sticks and stones, beat this national army and brought an end to the Diaz regime. The victors, as is customary, wrote the military history. They attributed their success against the hitherto invincible Diaz army to brilliant stratagems, heroic deeds, and superior fighting abilities, which overcame seemingly insuperable physical and technical military odds.[3]

Such an interpretation, though inspiring, was patently false.

Subsequent military history research cut through this revolutionary myth to reveal the vaunted Diaz army to have been in actuality but a fragile shell. When the insurgents forced the *federales* to take to the field, the latter's ineffectiveness was quickly revealed. Supply lines broke down immediately; shoddy hand-me-down European armaments functioned poorly; the National Arms Factory needed a month to produce a half-day's supply of ammunition. Only 12,000 troops, half the number on the muster rolls, could be readied for field operations in the spring of 1911, and only a fraction of these dared be committed to the insurrections in the remote north lest the capital itself became vulnerable to attack.[4]

The War Ministry staff, a corrupt bureaucracy that jockeyed for favours and position from the ageing dictator, studied the experience of the Franco-Prussian war in its strategy and planning. The top rank, division general, was still reserved for heroes of wars against the French occupation of 1862–7. Such generals, like Diaz himself, were all octogenarians by 1911. The most coveted rank for the career officer became *jefe* (colonel), nicknamed *las buscas* (perquisites), for this rank conveyed opportunities to pad muster rolls and to graft on food and supplies. Non-coms, whose main qualification was an ability to read and write, were demoralised by the corruption, irresponsibility, and indifference of the officers. Over fifty per cent of conscripts were illiterate Indians; most of the remainder were vagabonds, beggars, and criminals. When confronted with battle, these wretched ones deserted in droves.[5]

On the other hand, the insurgents, thanks to successful ambush tactics and heavy smuggling of arms across the US border, were soon equipped with Remington and Winchester rifles. Nearly all their troops were mounted, had the advantage of operating on friendly terrain, and avoided the long supply line problem by living off the countryside where they operated.[6] However, military historians concluded that the insurgents' triumph over the regular army in 1911 was attributable more to the weakness and collapse of the *federales* than it was to the strength and resourcefulness of the insurgents.[7] The 1911 revolutionary triumph resulted in a military compromise. In the interest of ending hostilities quickly and avoiding further bloodshed, President Madero agreed to disband the revolutionary forces in the Centre and South and incorporate those of the North with the old Federal Army into a new national army. The folly of this undertaking was revealed in General Victoriano Huerta's February 1913 *cuartelazo* (barracks coup) which deposed and murdered Madero.[8] This ended the military compromise. In the next sixteen months of battle the issue as to who was to govern Mexico, Huerta and the *federales* at the Centre or Venustiano Carranza and the revolutionary armies of the North, was to be decided.

Again the insurgency succeeded, this time leading to complete destruction of the federal army. Again, the victors supplied a military history myth — brilliant stratagems, extraordinary heroism, and superior will triumphed over seemingly impossible military odds. They wrote that Huerta's troops, weapons, and ammunition were overwhelming. General Miguel Sánchez Lamego, the brilliant military historian of this so-called Constitutionalist Revolution of 1913–14, set the record straight in 1957.[9] Though Huerta claimed an army of 70,000 on paper, in actuality he was unable to put half that many into the field. The *federales* did not outnumber the insurgents in a single major battle, and their troops totalled under 40,000 at the time of their surrender and disbandment in August of 1914. Unlike the 1911 insurgency, where ubiquitous guerrilla bands simply overwhelmed the numerical capacity of the *federales* to cope with them, the Constitutionalist insurgency of 1913–14 was decided in more conventional battlefield confrontations. The United States government's arming of the insurgents across the northern border while using its navy to blockade European arms shipments to the *federales* ensured Huerta's inevitable defeat.[10]

Mexico's regular army had now been destroyed, but in the process a number of insurgent armies had taken its place. True, these revolutionary armies had liberated the Mexican people from their traditional exploiters and rulers, but now it was going to be necessary to liberate the people from their liberators. This civil-military struggle for political supremacy, in the context of which the insurgency problem from 1915 to 1940 must be viewed, was to last a full quarter century, whereas the Revolution itself, from Madero's 1911 uprising to Carranza's 1914 triumph, had consumed only three and a half years. Almost immediately the victorious revolutionary generals began squabbling over the political spoils. In the last quarter of 1914 and the first quarter of 1915, Pancho Villa's mighty revolutionary Army of the North challenged Carranza, who barely won with the loyal support of Alvaro Obregón's Army of the Northwest and Pablo González's Army of the Northeast. During this chaotic half-year, Mexico City was alternately occupied by government and insurgent forces no less than half a dozen times.[11]

The elimination of the Villa threat by 1916 made Carranza's supremacy far from absolute. For this bloody internecine struggle against Villa and Emiliano Zapata had been won with a large number of improvised state and provincial generals, each of whom now exercised a high degree of local autonomy. In essence, Mexican politics had retrogressed to pre-Diaz conditions; the central government had again lost control over the outlying states. When the Diaz regime collapsed and the subsequent social revolution destroyed the Federal army, the military condition of the states changed from satrapies held in bondage to the Federal government by regular army officers loyal to the dictator into autonomous fiefs ruled by amateur generals of the revolution.[12] This fragmented power condition was to be the root of the insurgency problem in Mexico for the next twenty-five years. In 1916, the defeated *Villistas* and *Zapatistas* reverted to guerrilla warfare and harassed the Mexican countryside throughout Carranza's four years in the presidency. The utter inability of Mexico's revolutionary armies to control insurgency was clearly demonstrated in early 1916 when Villa's embittered forces invaded the state of New Mexico, an outrage which brought General John J. Pershing's punitive retaliatory expedition of 10,000 US troops into northern Mexico for a full year.[13] This chronic insurgency was an inevitable by-product of Mexico's great social cataclysm. The centrifugal force of revolutionary violence in the years 1911–15 had fragmented the unified military and political basis of national power which Diaz had constructed. To cope effectively with the resultant chaos what Mexico needed was a coalescence of the popular forces that had been spawned by the revolution, namely labour, the peasantry, and the revolutionary armies.

Over the course of a full generation, from 1920 to 1940, three great revolutionary generals, Alvaro Obregón, Plutarco Elias Calles, and Lázaro Cárdenas, gradually achieved this difficult triumph of revolutionary nationalism. In the process, the insurgency problem was finally brought under control. General Alvaro Obregón, commander of the Revolutionary Army of the Northwest, conqueror of Villa, War Minister under Carranza and soon his political rival, initiated the process. Between the years 1917 and 1920, while military-political *caudillo* in his native state of Sonora in northwest Mexico, he began to establish a national political network which would facilitate his ascension to the presidency as the people's choice in the elections scheduled for the summer of 1920. With a strong background of popular support founded on his heroic military image and his political stance as defender of the social goals of the revolutions, he was able to consolidate power on the basis of the agrarian and labour movements, linked politically with him through members of the revolutionary army.[14]

Thus, the year 1920 became the turning point in the century-long history of insurgency in Mexico. The military showdown of that year was between Carranza, with his regional military *caudillos* on the one hand, and Obregón with his national peasant, labour, and military forces, on the other. The triumph of the latter in the key Agua Prieta Revolution of April 1920 was the last successful insurgency in Mexico's history. It marked the decisive triumph of social revolutionary nationalism over regional militarism.[15] Although no Mexican government has been overthrown by force since 1920, this is not to say that insurgency was suddenly no longer a serious problem. The fact is that it was just barely beaten in 1920 and that one of the central government's principal political tasks for the next generation was to wear it down gradually but steadily until it was finally destroyed in the year 1940.

It will be instructive to examine a bit more closely this counter-insurgency process. It has two key features: (1) for the regular army it meant disciplining, nationalising, professionalising, depoliticising, and weakening it; (2) for labour and the peasantry it meant organising and strengthening them politically on a national basis and building them up into para-military counterpoises strong enough to resist the supremacy of the regular army. Once in power, Obregón first began to develop the civilian counterpoises necessary to protect himself against the military opposition his planned army reforms were almost certain to provoke. For its critical support in the 1920 rebellion, labour was rewarded by implementing, for the first time, the labour reforms in the 1917 Constitution – the right to strike, the right to organise, the right to minimum wages. In return, the Labour Party provided Obregón with his principal support in Congress, and organised labour founded a workers' militia to defend his administration. When the new labour bosses became increasingly hard to handle, Obregón turned to the peasantry for added support. To this end he began to redistribute land to the needy who responded by forming a pro-Obregón peasant political party and a nationwide organisation of rural militias superior in numbers to the regular army.[16]

Concurrently, Obregón began to tackle the army problem. The first task was to cashier all the *Carranista* officers and to buy off Pancho Villa and the *Zapatistas*. Next, he began to incorporate the regional revolutionary generals into the regular army by putting them all on the federal payroll. This was the old Diaz tactic of granting them material gain in exchange for surrender of their political independence. Meanwhile, he reopened the *Colegio Militar* and began to train and develop a corps of young professional officers for a future national army. Finally, he reduced the size of the army one half (from 100,000 to 50,000) and cut its share of the national budget from two-thirds to one-third of the total.[17] The ever-growing military opposition to such drastic reforms resulted in the December 1923 army insurgency, known as the de la Huerta revolt. Over half the army, both officers and men, defected and very nearly toppled the government. It was only the fighting support of peasant and labour militia that enabled Obregón to turn the tide in 1924 and transfer the presidency to his designated successor, General Calles, [18]

General Calles, Mexico's most durable revolutionary strongman, held sway for a full decade. A radical socialist reformer, he was determined to deepen the social revolution. Calles' main political prop became organised labour. Luis Morones became Minister of Labour and his Regional Confederation of Mexican Labour, over one million strong, began to reap vast privileges and material benefits from the new pro-labour president. The peasants were by no means forgotten, for Calles doubled the pace of land reform to benefit thousands of rural villagers. The victims of such reforms were the propertied elements. Businessmen, both foreign and domestic, were obligated to improve the lot of their employees, and the landlords to give up their idle lands to the needy.[19]

Insurgency, under Calles, first came from the Catholic Church. It was deliberately provoked by the President in 1926 when he began to enforce the anti-clerical provisions of the 1917 Constitution by closing church schools, deporting foreign priests, and requiring civil registry for all church authorities. The clergy responded by stopping religious services and closing down the churches. Calles countered by moving cannons in front of the church doors to keep them open. Catholic partisans resorted to violence in the various states of southwestern Mexico. Priests and Catholic laymen there organised armed bands, the so-called *Cristeros*, who roamed the countryside burning public schools, killing teachers, and dynamiting trains. By early 1927 the *Cristero* insurgents, led by former Federal Army generals, had over 12,000 men in the field.

Calles responded by sending in the regular army. For every school burned a Church was looted; for every teacher murdered a priest lost his life. Captured *Cristero* insurgents were hung by their necks on long lines of telephone poles. The army was more than a match for the insurgents whose main forces were decimated and scattered by the end of 1927. Army patrols spent the next two years stamping out the remaining guerrilla bands. By the end of 1929 it was all over. The army

had triumphed in a brutal application of superior force. The Church
surrendered, and henceforth complied with the iron law of revolutionary
government.[20]

The regular army's impressive counter-insurgency capability was
evidence of the success of continuing military reforms. Credit for trans-
forming Mexico's army into a truly national, professional organisation
must go largely to Calles' War Minister, General Joaquín Amaro. He
began his reforms in the ranks by improving recruiting standards,
military equipment, and training programmes. He streamlined and
professionalised the *Colegio Militar* and carefully screened the new
cadets. The best young officers he sent for advanced training to US,
French and Spanish military academies. He weeded out the amateurs;
once more reduced the size of the army to 50,000 (from the 75,000
to which it had expanded to combat the de la Huerta insurgency of
1923), and he cut its budget by one-third.[21]

The question now was would this lean, compact, more efficient
armed force be capable of dealing with another military insurgency —
namely, a new challenge from the increasingly disgruntled revolutionary
generals and their private armies? The issue was drawn in the Gómez
military insurgency of 1927 and the Escobar rebellion of 1929. In
both cases, as in 1923—4, the hastily called-up peasant and labour
militias swung the balance in favour of the government. The success of
the Obregón-Calles reforms is revealed in the declining magnitude of
army defections. In 1923, more than half joined the insurgency. In
1927 and 1929, less than a quarter did so.[22]

The days of the amateur revolutionary generals and their regional
military insurgents were now numbered. It was Calles' hand-picked
successor, General Lázaro Cárdenas, who delivered the *coup de grace*.
First, he turned on Calles himself, next on Amaro, and then against
the other prominent political generals who still held the top political
and military posts in the nation. He began taking away their military
commands and disbanding their private armies. When they resisted he
forced them into exile. This was the fate of Calles and a number of his
supportive generals in 1936. The last serious insurgency in Mexican
history broke out in 1938, when General Saturnino Cedillo, long-time
regional *caudillo* of the state of San Luis Potosi, resisted the nationalis-
ation of his private army of 10,000. Provoked to violence, the national
army crushed them in a few weeks, then ambushed and gunned down
Cedillo himself.[23]

Cárdenas' aim was no less than to render the army completely
apolitical, to reduce it to a small, disciplined, professional, domestic

order-keeping force that would never again interfere with revolutionary reforms nor have the capability to challenge popular-backed political leadership. To this end, in 1938 he reorganised the national revolutionary party into four sectors – labour, peasant, popular, and military. The effect of this was to reduce the army sector, which had hitherto dominated the presidential selection process, to a permanent minority position in the voting as the other three now controlled the party. Then he continued to expand the para-military popular counterpoises while also continuing to reduce the size and budget of the regular army. Both labour and peasant militias far exceeded the regular army in troop strength by the late 1930s.[24]

The election of 1940 was the last gasp of hitherto politically dominant revolutionary generals. Thirty-four of them took leave from active service to back their candidate, General Andreu Almazán, in his challenge to Cárdenas' man, General Avila Cammacho. It was no contest. The labour-peasant backed official party overwhelmed the revolutionary generals and their conservative backers. Almazán's threat to lead a new insurgency came to naught.[25] The political shift was complete. The generals of the revolution were out of it. No military man was ever again elected president of Mexico. No more uprisings by regional caudillism. No more military defections. No more attempted coups. As of 1940, military insurgency, actual or threatened, the scourge of Mexican domestic politics since the beginnings of its national history in 1810, was finally dead. It had been overwhelmed by triumphant revolutionary nationalism. Since 1940, the Mexican government has been controlled by civilian authorities supported by mass-based and armed popular forces. And yet, despite the domestic calm of the past thirty-eight years, can one aver that the problem of insurgency and the regular army has forever ended in Mexico? Probably not.

Potential trouble springs from the fact that since 1940 the old national revolutionary consensus has progressively broken down. Political consolidation and economic development resulted in the peasant-labour social revolution being overlapped by a capitalist industrial revolution. Though the revolutionary party continues to overwhelm its opposition in elections, that party is no longer revolutionary. The revolution is dead. Social and political power in Mexico has shifted from the masses to the middle classes, or the bourgeoisie. Ever since World War II, the Mexican government has placed its policy priorities upon economic development rather than social change. Land reform has stopped. Labour's share of the economy has grown ever smaller. Peasant and worker leaders no longer represent constituents. They have been co-opted by the middle-class dominated ruling party.[26]

As a result, the frustrations of the masses have become increasingly visible over the past generation. During the late 1950s, the regular army was frequently called out to curb sporadic labour violence. In 1968, thousands of army troops had to be brought in to quell the leftist student riots at the National University, in which 100 to 200 died. In 1977, thousands of troops were rushed to the Pacific coast state of Sinaloa to halt the peasant land seizures there. The regular army has shown an impressive capability to handle this kind of sporadic, localised, popular violence. The question arises as to whether it would be able to do so if it became ubiquitous.

Mexico's regular armed forces number 70,000, hardly an impressive force for a nation whose population is nearing 70 million. The rural militias are twice this size, but could they be relied on to co-operate with the army and come to the government's aid, as in the past, if the main issue was the growing land hunger, poverty, and frustration of the rural masses? Also, the high insurgency potential resulting from Mexican geography has not been radically altered by advances in counter-insurgency technology. In addition, urban insurgency could become a threat. Accelerated farm to city migration is producing huge, increasingly unmanageable urban concentrations, with Mexico City destined to become the world's largest city in another decade if present demographic trends continue.

Reducing Mexico's explosive population growth rate would help ameliorate the problem. Effectively sealing the United States border against illegal migrants would seriously aggravate it. If present demographic and illegal migration trends continue, however, whether or not insurgency becomes a serious problem for the regular army of Mexico in the foreseeable future will pretty much depend upon whether economic growth is sufficiently rapid to keep rising mass social frustrations from exploding again into widespread violence.

Notes

1. Carlton Beals, *Porfirio Diaz* (Lippencott, Philadephia, 1932), pp. 223–55, 287–9.

2. Thomas A. Janvier, 'The Mexican Army', *Armies of Today* (New York, 1893), pp. 366–96; Charles M. Jerram, *Armies of the World* (London, 1899), pp. 206–7, 299; Percy F. Martin, *Mexico in the Twentieth Century* (Edward Arnold, London, 1907, 2 vols.), vol. 2, pp. 42–3.

3. Alfonso Tarracena, *Mi vida en el vertigo de la revolución mejicana* (Mexico, DF, 1936), pp. 342–5; Jesus Silva Herzog, *Un ensayo sobre la*

revolución mejicana (Mexico, DF, 1946), pp. 28–9.

4. Jorge Vera Estanol, *La revolución mejicana: origenes y resultados* (Mexico, DF, 1957), pp. 48–53.

5. Ibid.; Ernest Gruening, *Mexico and Its Heritage* (Appleton, New York, 1928), pp. 301–2.

6. Charles Cumberland, *The Mexican Revolution: Genesis under Madero* (University of Texas Press, Austin, 1952), pp. 144–5.

7. Vera Estanol, *La revolución mejicana*, pp. 48–53; Juan Barragon Rodriguez, *Historia de ejército de la Revolución Constitucionalista* (Mexico, DF, 1946, 2 vols.), vol. 1, pp. 17–88.

8. Manuel González Ramirez, *La revolución social en Mejico* (Mexico, DF, 1960–6, 3 vols.), vol. 1, pp. 244–6; Cumberland, *The Mexican Revolution*, pp. 159–160.

9. See his *Historia Militar de la revolución constitutionalista* (Mexico, DF, 1956–60, 5 vols.).

10. Barragon Rodrignez, *Historia de ejército de la Revolución Constitutiönalista*, vol. 1.

11. Ibid., vol. 2.

12. Edwin Lieuwen, *Mexican Militarism: the Political Rise and Fall of the Revolutionary Army, 1910–1940* (University of New Mexico Press, Albuquerque, 1968), pp. 27–40.

13. See Clarence C. Clenendon, *The United States and Pancho Villa* (Cornell University Press, Ithaca, 1961).

14. Linda Hall, 'Alvaro Obregón and the Mexican Revolution, 1912–1920' (Unpublished PhD dissertation, Columbia University, New York, 1976), pp. 1–28.

15. John W. Dulles, *Yesterday in Mexico* (University of Texas Press, Austin, 1961), pp. 31–54.

16. Ibid., pp. 93–144.

17. Lieuwen, *Mexican Militarism*, pp. 61–71.

18. Dulles, *Yesterday in Mexico*, pp. 218–60; Gruening, *Mexico and its Heritage*, pp. 322–3.

19. Dulles, *Yesterday in Mexico*, pp. 217–95.

20. See David D. Bailey, *Viva Crito Rey: the Cristero Rebellion and the Church-State Conflict in Mexico* (University of Texas Press, Austin, 1974).

21. Carlton Beals, 'The Indian Who Sways Mexico's Destiny', *New York Times*, 7 December 1930, sec. 5, p. 8.

22. Lieuwen, *Mexican Militarism*, pp. 95–104.

23. Ibid., pp. 121–8.

24. Frank Brandenberg, *The Making of Modern Mexico* (Prentice Hall, Engelwood Cliffs, 1964), pp. 89–99.

25. See Marta Hunt, 'The Mexican Election of 1940' (unpublished MA thesis, University of New Mexico, Albuquerque, 1962).

26. See Roger D. Hansen, *The Politics of Mexican Development* (Johns Hopkins Press, Baltimore, 1971).

3 THE IRISH INSURGENCY, 1918–21: THE MILITARY PROBLEM

Charles Townshend

Between early 1919 and mid-1921, the British military and police authorities in Ireland faced an armed conflict which was quite outside the range of their experience. In the years following the apparently abortive 1916 Rebellion, these authorities had rested secure in the belief that, as one military intelligence officer put it: 'The presence of the military and the rapid dispersal of all armed bodies in the past rebellion have put an end to all hope of success by armed opposition in the future, and the extremists recognize this.'[1] Few, if any, senior officials had even a vague suspicion that would-be rebels might in future adopt a strategy of survival rather than one of martyrdom in open battle.

The Republican guerrilla campaign which began in 1919 was more inventive, resilient and efficient than any previous Irish resistance movement. It developed on two distinct levels, indicated at the start, on 21 January 1919, by the meeting of the first Republican parliament, Dáil Eireann, which issued a unilateral Declaration of Independence and prepared to establish an alternative system of government and the (fortuitously) simultaneous mounting of the first ambush and killing of police by Irish Volunteers at Soloheadbeg, county Tipperary. The activities of the military group developed fairly slowly, and during 1918–19 were mostly limited to the formation of local forces and the securing of arms through small raids and attacks. For some time, the political group, Sinn Féin, forming the majority of Dáil Eireann, and following the non-violent ideas of Arthur Griffith (whose model can be characterised as one of civil resistance), was visibly reluctant to accept the 'physical force' methods adopted by the more ardent spirits of the Volunteers, and concentrated on the subversion of British governmental institutions.[2]

The British government itself ignored this potential divergence of opinion in the ranks of its enemies, and in the autumn of 1919 it imposed an impartial proscription on Sinn Féin, the Irish Volunteers, and Dáil Eireann. This blanket action naturally tended to push moderates into the arms of extremists — heirs to the traditional belief that only naked physical compulsion would induce Britain to grant Ireland self-government. This belief was considerably reinforced by the obvious diffidence with which the government took up the thorny problem of Home Rule at the end of the Great War.

The impacting of opposition did not mean, however, that the government held an exaggerated view of the strength of its opponents. The reverse was rather the case. All the evidence suggests that the full seriousness of the Republican challenge was not appreciated in London until 1921, and during the two preceding years it was met by a succession of half-measures. The Imperial government (as distinct from the Irish government, or executive, in Dublin) was habitually myopic in the Irish direction, and showed a sustained reluctance to accept that the Republican movement was assaulting the whole foundation of British rule. In this reluctance it was undoubtedly encouraged by the slowness with which the subversive campaign developed. It is quite clear that the emergence of armed struggle was much more ragged, sporadic and inconsistent than Republican accounts have led most subsequent writers to believe. The primary barrier to the creation of an effective counter-insurgency policy was, and remained, the difficulty of identifying that an insurgency in fact existed.

This of course raises the question whether an insurgency did exist, and calls for definition of the term. I take it to signify a sustained level of armed opposition to government, sufficient to prevent the normal exercise of administrative and legal authority. At its most sophisticated it will have a clear political programme, and a definite framework of technical military (usually guerrilla) methods. It need not be so sophisticated, however. More primitive insurgency was to some extent endemic in Ireland, and until the later nineteenth century it had not been uncommon for large tracts of country to pass outside police control for months at a time. The conflict which took shape after 1916 bore strong traces of traditional agrarian violence, and it is by no means easy to see at which point a characteristically modern guerrilla war emerged.[3] A clear enough political message, national independence, was propounded by Sinn Féin, but despite its ideological vagueness (carefully avoiding divisive issues) it took some time to gain widespread acceptance — and indeed was explicitly rejected in the northeast. Even in the nationalist south there was little agreement about the form which national independence should take. The shooting war was conducted by a small group of outright republicans who had at first no substantial popular backing; the sort of incidents which occurred reflected their weakness.

The overriding objective of most local Volunteer groups was always to obtain arms, and early raids were aimed exclusively at this.[4] The easiest targets were the 'big fellas', landowners who kept revolvers and shotguns in their houses, but if more serious weapons were wanted, the optimum target was the Royal Irish Constabulary (RIC), an armed, semi-military gendarmerie distributed in small, indefensible posts.[5] A combination of boycott and physical attacks forced the RIC to concentrate in large sections (of around 12 men) during the winter of 1919–20, a retreat which reduced both their own effectiveness and the prestige of the administration. The Volunteers, however, were henceforth faced with more formidable objectives, which they had to tackle by means of night attacks (since they were still a part-time force). A number of these attacks were pressed with determination, and 12 posts were captured or destroyed in the first six months of 1920.[6] At the same time the operation of the legal system was undermined by intimidation of witnesses and juries on a scale previously unknown, even in Ireland. The summer assizes of 1920 offered the government the humiliating spectacle of white gloves (the sign that no criminal cases were being brought) being handed to judges in counties where armed raids were almost daily occurrences. By this time there was some sort of Volunteer (or Irish Republican Army) formation in every county, though their strength and effectiveness varied.[7] Cork had three well-organised brigades, each mustering several hundred reliable men and perhaps a hundred rifles, whereas a county such as Sligo might produce no more than a couple of dozen men and a few shotguns. Such wild inconsistencies underlined the traditional, territorial nature of the IRA. Its headquarters staff in Dublin, headed by Richard Mulcahy and Michael Collins, might develop a fairly sophisticated theory of guerrilla war, but it could never impose a blueprint on the whole organisation.[8]

It may therefore be said that the basis of the insurgency was a good deal narrower than was suggested by the very active and successful Republican publicity department. Nonetheless, there is no doubt that in the south-west the defiance of law was sufficiently sustained to be deemed insurgency, had the government been psychologically prepared to see it as such. The official view, however, while recognising the existence of a state of disorder (in itself a not altogether unwelcome pretext for postponing constitutional reform), was that it did not stem from widespread or deep-seated popular antagonism. A concise statement of the government's analysis was produced at an important Cabinet meeting on 31 May 1920 by the Chief Secretary for Ireland, Hamar Greenwood:

The vital point is to deal with the Thugs, a number of whom are going about shooting in Dublin, Limerick and Cork. We are certain that these are handsomely paid . . . The community is hostile, indifferent or terrorised. The majority I believe are terrorised.[9]

This may conveniently be labelled the 'murder gang theory'. It exercised a strong influence on British policy throughout the conflict, though it was not universally accepted, even in Cabinet. The most notable dissentient was Lord French, Lord Lieutenant of Ireland from 1918 to 1921, and a member of the Cabinet from October 1919. French believed that the whole Irish Volunteer movement must be made the objective, and be crushed by mass arrests, together with the application of martial law in disturbed areas. In this, however, he was opposed by his own executive in Dublin. The use of martial law was vetoed by the Viceregal Council in October 1919, and the next month the senior officers of the Crown forces in Ireland assured the Cabinet that all that was needed was a small number of exemplary sentences on extremists.[10] This idea was accepted gratefully by the Cabinet, and maintained throughout 1920 in the teeth of accumulating evidence that Irish opposition was far too extensive to be intimidated, and that the supposed moderate majority (whose existence and nature had never been investigated) was a figment of the imagination.

British military policy in Ireland thus developed in an atmosphere of political hesitancy. This had particular effect with regard to the police force, which, as we have seen, had been thrown on the defensive by the beginning of 1920. There were in fact fears that it was on the brink of collapse.[11] Partly in desperation, to grasp at any available force with which to maintain order, and partly out of a desire to keep the civil police in the forefront of the conflict, the RIC was reinforced from January onwards by ex-servicemen recruited in Britain. These 'Black and Tans' were quite unlike the normal personnel of the RIC: foreigners, without long-term career prospects in the force, habituated to excitement and violence, they had little chance of restoring the RIC's normal relationship with the Irish community. They symbolised the militarisation of the constabulary, yet at no time were they placed under military control and discipline. The dichotomy between the police and the army, preventing the establishment of a unified command structure and creating damaging friction at all levels, was to be a constant feature in the chequered pattern of military involvement in Ireland.

In the spring of 1920 an attempt was made to rationalise the legendary confusion of Dublin Castle and regenerate the administration. For two years, Lord French had been urging the creation of a single strong executive, and at last, following the appointment in April of a new Chief Secretary, Sir Hamar Greenwood, and a new Commander-in-Chief, Sir Nevil Macready, a committee of investigation ordered a transfusion of senior personnel from Whitehall to Dublin.[12] At the same time Macready, who had (with unfortunate consequences) refused the overall command of troops and police, made a cursory investigation into the RIC and the other Irish police force, the unarmed Dublin Metropolitan Police.[13] He concluded that they were 'hopelessly out of date', and that a new officer must be brought in to take control of them.[14] To the new Under-Secretary at Dublin Castle, Sir John Anderson, he indicated that the RIC would be better off if it were disarmed, but he did not press this view; nor was he able to secure the appointment of his own nominee as chief of police, a post eventually given to Major-General H.H. Tudor.[15]

Although he was a serving military officer, Tudor threw himself wholeheartedly into the task of rebuilding the RIC, and also of preserving its independent powers of action. The consequences of his policy were far-reaching. The RIC had, to all intents, already lost its effectiveness as a civil police force. Tudor continued its policy of withdrawal and concentration in defensible barracks, and also stepped up the recruitment of ex-servicemen. The force thereby lost any of its remaining 'civil' characteristics: with remarkable candour Tudor told the Cabinet in July that 'as a police force' the RIC could not last much longer, but 'they might have a great affect as a military body'.[16] The Cabinet found nothing strange in this, and saw no reason to ask why in this case the RIC should be preferable to the army itself. Still more eloquent of political attitudes was the enthusiasm with which Tudor's announcement that he was recruiting a new force composed of ex-officers was received.

This latter corps, afterwards called the Auxiliary Division of the RIC (ADRIC), was inaugurated on 27 July. It was formed of independent, fully motorised companies of around 100 men each, and its creation was an outright repudiation of the conclusion earlier reached by a military committee (set up by the Cabinet in May) that any new forces raised for Ireland should be military ones. The Auxiliary companies were self-conscious elite units, brooking little control from either the military or the civil power. They had obvious potential for counter-insurgency operations, but most of them frittered it away through inadequate training and, above all, inadequate discipline.[17] As with the

Black and Tan recruits in the regular RIC, the mild constabulary discipline was sadly inappropriate for these young war veterans placed in a
situation of intense strain and provocation. This danger had been
clearly stated, not only by the army, but also by the former head of the
RIC.[18]

Tudor was not, as has sometimes been suggested, given a completely
free hand, but he had political backing in his policy of expanding and
militarising the RIC, and also in his charitable attitude to the illegal
acts which resulted from its indiscipline. Such backing came from the
inner Cabinet rather than the Irish executive, which by July 1920 had
substantially turned against Tudor's ideas.[19] The critical issue was the
illegal retaliation, or reprisals, which began to mount in frequency
during the summer. Although troops and police were equally guilty of
such reprisals, the attitudes of their chiefs were very different.
Macready's determination to control retaliation, by all means short of
breaking the spirit of his troops, was evident from his special General
Order of 17 August.[20] Tudor, on the other hand, more fearful for his
men's morale, never directly forbade illegal retaliation. After six
months during which only a couple of half-hearted warnings emerged
from the Constabular Office to set against the inflammatory exhortations
of the RIC *Weekly Summary*, Sir John Anderson came to the conclusion
that although 'in private conversation Tudor would agree that steps
ought to be taken to deal with these (serious breaches of discipline). . .
he took another line when he met his men'.[21] Quarrels over discipline
afflicted the British authorities throughout the war, quite apart from
the matter of the effect of reprisals on the British cause as a whole.
Distrust of Tudor and his political backers, particularly Churchill,
created an unfortunate atmosphere for the prosecution of a complex
and sensitive conflict.

Political ambiguity and executive disunity were the foundations of
the military campaign. Their most noticeable consequence was the
failure to define the role of the military forces. During the winter of
1919–20 it had become evident that the RIC was incapable of handling
even the limited offensive which had so far been developed by the IRA.
Indeed, over the previous year it had been necessary for the police to
call in military support in several counties, which had been declared
Special Military Areas under the Defence of the Realm Act. At last, on
7 January 1920, orders were issued 'to transfer to the Competent
Military Authority the powers, previously vested in the police authorities
and magistrates, of instituting and organising action against the per-
petrators of outrage and the organisers of lawlessness'.[22] The military

authorities thereupon drew up, in consultation with the RIC, lists of wanted men in each divisional area, and prepared a programme of raids, searches and arrests to be carried out on 30 January. Internment camps were designated. On the 20th, however, the original deportation warrants issued to the divisions (80 to 5th Division in the south) were withdrawn, and a system substituted whereby the Dublin Castle law department assessed all cases after the arrests had been carried out.[23] The inevitable result of this was that many of the arrested men were subsequently released, reducing the psychological effect of the sweep.

Nonetheless, the military programme went ahead on the night of 30 January, when 57 out of 74 men sought were arrested; and by 14 April, 317 known or suspected IRA officers and men had been taken. The RIC accompanied the troops on raids, but their assistance was not highly valued by the army, and it is not surprising that the Inspector General of the RIC thought, as he told the Fisher committee in May, that 'contrary to the expressed view of the Military, the latter were not assisting the police, but that the reverse was the case'.[24] The army was particularly dissatisfied with what it saw as the incompetence of the police intelligence system, which was producing little worthwhile information, and which was in any case not constructed on any principles comprehensible to military intelligence officers.[25] A new military intelligence service had to be built up from scratch, a truly daunting task which was never to be fully accomplished. Still, during the first three months of 1920 it appeared that the army was gradually and logically taking over the maintenance – or attempted maintenance – of law and order. With the reforms of April and May, however, this process was curtailed. On 3 May the legal powers vested in the military authorities were removed, and raids, arrests and internment were sharply cut back.[26] Greenwood embarked on a policy of conciliation, and Macready brought the army into a 'low profile' stance, impressing on his generals 'the importance of taking no measures that may cause irritation'. Macready himself was a convinced Home Ruler and saw nothing but increased bitterness, and possible complete disaster, resulting from strong military action.[27] Throughout the summer the army soft-pedalled while the RIC built up its strength. Both of them favoured the principle of concentration in defensible centres from which patrols would sweep the countryside, and consequently demanded vast increases in motor transport. These appeared only slowly – faster for the police than for the troops, because of the army's rapid reversion to peacetime red tape.[28] The principle of mobility was perhaps initially adopted *faute de mieux*, to offset shortage of troops, but it soon turned into a principle in its own right. Lord Carson's objection that 'in the past it had been impossible to control disturbances from the centre' was ignored, even though all that Macready could offer was the rather vague hope that 'by moving about the country (the troops) may from time to time surprise the Sinn Féin bands'.[29] The Chief of the Imperial General Staff (CIGS), Wilson, condemned this idea as 'useless', but it was enthusiastically supported by Greenwood, and it entirely suited the outlook of the Cabinet. It was not until the spring of 1921 that some of the front-line troops began to realise that motor transport was too clumsy to achieve surprise under normal Irish conditions. It is possible that some of the senior commands never realised it.

It is true that the army's numerical weakness militated against methods involving closer control. The Special Military Areas set up in 1918–19 had each required a war-strength battalion; by 1920 the level of disorder had risen, and the strength of battalions had fallen. Irish Command had at its disposal only 29 battalions, few of them with more than 500 bayonets (i.e. effective infantry), and many with far fewer. The pattern of demobilisation had stripped this command of its veterans, and after the war Ireland rapidly reverted, in the War Office mind, to its former status as a training area. Drafts to overseas units continually pared away the most experienced men, and in any case the standard of the postwar recruits, both officers and other ranks, was not high.[30] It was thus a raw and under-strength army which faced the complex and demanding Irish security problem. Even in January 1921, when strength had risen to 51 battalions, Macready warned the Cabinet that the strain of incessant security duties (guards, patrols, raids) on top of normal and essential military training, was continuing to have a deleterious effect.[31]

To this military strength the RIC added in mid-1920 some 10,100 men, a total which fell gradually to just over 9,900 in September, and then rose again to 11,000 in late October, 12,000 in mid-December and 13,000 in January 1921. The ADRIC became operational in September with five companies totalling 478 men, a muster which rose to eleven companies and nearly 1,000 men by December.[32] During the summer the superstructure of the RIC was modified, and the old rank of Divisional Commissioner restored (seven for the whole of Ireland), ostensibly in the hope of improving coordination both within the RIC and between it and the army. In neither was there conspicuous success; several of the Divisional Commissioners turned into satraps as independent as the ADRIC companies they sought to control.

The summer of 1920 was a period of stalemate. In July, a major
military conference at General Headquarters (GHQ) in Kilmainham
produced no tactical ideas, and Macready could only report to the
government that

> while we cannot during the last four months show any definite
> gain for the number of troops and transport that have been sent
> over, matters would have been a great deal worse if we had not
> been so reinforced.[33]

From the General Officer Commanding (GOC) 5th Division, Sir Hugh
Jeudwine, Macready received on 23 July a depressing appreciation of
developments since April. Jeudwine declared that the situation had
'altered considerably for the worse', owing largely to the increased
efficiency of the rebels and to the transport crisis caused by the
refusal of Irish railway workers to convey armed troops or
munitions. British policy as a whole, he added, was 'drifting without
any settled course or goal'.[34] As if to demonstrate this point, a
Cabinet conference on the same day revealed deep divergencies
between the ideas of the governments in London and Dublin, the
police, and the military authorities. This was in fact the first full
discussion that the Cabinet had held on the Irish crisis, and Ireland
continued to occupy a peripheral place in its attentions. (It is useful to
recall that the Spa Conference had just ended the week before.)
Greenwood produced a measure which was in essence a compromise
between the Cabinet's fears of public opinion, and the ultimate logical
necessity of outright military rule. The Restoration of Order in Ireland
Act (which was rushed through Parliament early in August) once more
extended the legal powers of the military authorities, as well as the
jurisdiction of courts-martial. However, the army was still prevented
from mounting a full-scale programme of raids and arrests, and from
controlling the police. The Act reflected the persistence of the belief
that a few capital sentences would suffice to break the Republican
spirit, and its main object was to sidestep the ordinary civil courts,
which had been rendered ineffectual by IRA intimidation. In this
object it succeeded, and the number of criminal convictions began
steadily to rise.

Capital convictions remained unforthcoming, however, while the
Act had another, unforeseen, consequence.[35] A greatly increased
number of IRA men were forced to go 'on the run', and in effect to
become full-time fighters. The first IRA 'Active Service Units', or

flying columns, began to form in August and September, a tactical development of considerable importance. The 'mobile' policy of the Crown forces had always suffered from limitations: motorised patrols sweeping through hostile country had only a transient pacifying effect, and one that was confined to the vicinity of the usable roads. Now, with the appearance of rebel flying columns, the patrols themselves were put at risk. In theory, the concentration of the rebels in larger and more permanent formations furnished better targets for military action, but in practice the IRA's grass-roots intelligence system and its ruthless terrorism against 'spies and informers' tended to offset this. Even when columns could be located, the most that troops usually achieved was to disperse, rather than pin down and destroy them.

The first dramatic outcome of this development was the ambush of a police patrol at Rineen, County Clare, on 20 September. A District Inspector and five constables were killed, allegedly with dumdum ammunition.[36] Next day a group of police carried out one of the most violent of all reprisals, ranging through the neighbouring towns of Ennistymon, Lahinch, and Milltown Malbay, killing four people and burning 26 buildings. This, together with the less destructive but better publicised reprisal at Balbriggan in county Meath, raised the war of terror and counter-terror to a new level. The system of 'unauthorised' or 'unofficial' reprisals, publicly disavowed but privately countenanced by the Cabinet, was an indication of the bankruptcy of British policy – not only that of Whitehall, but also that of the Irish forces. The army detested reprisals because they were 'unauthorised' and therefore subversive of discipline. But Macready was aware that a unit which did not react when provoked would be fatally lacking in spirit, and that moreover, as he pointed out to Wilson, 'where reprisals have taken place the whole atmosphere of the surrounding district has changed from one of hostility to one of cringing submission'.[37] People were even beginning to give information to the Crown forces. As a result, the army proposed an opportunistic compromise with its principles, the adoption of 'authorised' or 'official' reprisals, to be carried out under a publicly announced scheme and proper military control. The Cabinet, however, refused to countenance this idea, Lloyd George making it quite clear that the destruction of property (which the military scheme would involve) was politically much more unattractive than the shooting, with or without trial of known or suspected rebels.[38]

It is a striking fact that, apart from this proposal, the army had no clearcut plans for dealing with the crisis. The vagueness of military thinking was evident in a scheme submitted to the Cabinet on 26 September, proposing the 'clearance' of Ireland area by area, but offering no indication of how such an ambitious project could be accomplished with the troops available.[39] How were the areas to be cordoned off? How were they to be swept? After the sweep, even if successful, how were they to be kept clear? The army lacked not only the numbers, but also the techniques for such operations. Its state of training was poor at the beginning of the year, and did not markedly improve thereafter.[40] The clear lesson of the raids which formed the bulk of positive military operations during this period was that infantry units neither possessed, nor seemed able to acquire, adequate skills in searching buildings or vehicles. In a typical reproof delivered to a unit whose checkpoint had allegedly 'searched' a car four times without discovering two revolvers lying on the seat by the driver, 6th Division complained that 'it is evident that the Officers and NCOs do not realize the importance of the duties they are carrying out, and consequently treat such matters too lightly'.[41] As for searching large urban or rural areas for wanted men, an even more formidable disability was ever present — the lack of a reliable intelligence system.

The organisation of British intelligence in the Irish conflict is a subject which would require much fuller treatment than it can be given here. One of the primary aspects of counter-insurgency is that the need for information outweighs every other military factor. The Crown forces in Ireland, with a defective service of information, were fighting blindfold and with one hand tied behind their backs. Two types of information were needed, first, basic intelligence concerning the organisation of the IRA forces and the identity of their members, and second, operational intelligence, 'hot' information about their movements and present positions. Lack of the latter meant that searches and patrols would operate by pure chance, striking more often than not in the air. Lack of the former meant that even when the right spot was struck, the enemy might not be identified. Modern counter-insurgency thinking lays stress on the complex inter-relationship of overall policy, types of information, and methods of securing it: Kitson has suggested the importance of an intuitive grasp, on the part of company officers, of what he calls the 'development' of 'background' into 'contact' information.[42] Such a fluid concept was quite foreign to the army of 1920. In irregular warfare, the paramount problem for the regular force is to locate the enemy. It is an important problem in regular warfare as well, but one which had been reduced to near insignificance between 1914 and 1918. There is no doubt that the Great War produced a crop of regimental officers with little capacity or inclination to grasp the potential of front-line intelligence imaginatively used.[43] In consequence, undue reliance was placed on such specialist intelligence services as could be built up.

These latter proved incapable of tackling the problem on a sufficient scale. The reasons were partly organisational and partly personal, but at root it was a matter of not applying sufficient resources to overcome the obstacle of a fairly efficient rebel system with patchy but substantial popular co-operation. The effectiveness of IRA intelligence has been wildly exaggerated by almost all writers on the conflict, but it can be said to have delivered the goods, in that, at least until the spring of 1921, it gave IRA units a definite edge in the battle of wits against their opponents. The delay in building up a functional counter to this was primarily due to the sheer difficulty of the task, but a certain responsibility also devolves upon the shoulders of the director of joint intelligence in Ireland, Colonel Ormonde Winter, whose idiosyncratic cloak-and-dagger approach prevented him from effectively marrying the work of the police and the military intelligence services. In addition, Dublin loomed too large in his consciousness (as it did for his counterpart, Michael Collins), and he neglected the less exciting business of building up a provincial organisation.[44]

The secret war of the two opposing intelligence services burst into public view with the events of 'Bloody Sunday', 21 November 1920. Although several of the assassinations carried out by the IRA missed their mark, the rest reduced the Dublin military special branch to 'temporary paralysis'. Indirectly they had a rather different effect. Both the government and the army were galvanised into a new seriousness of approach. It was only now, for instance, that all military personnel were ordered to live inside barracks, and all outside areas were, perhaps overdramatically, designated 'No Man's Land'. A huge programme of arrest and internment was authorised, over 500 men being seized within a week.[45] Military morale rocketed. Mark Sturgis, Anderson's joint assistant Under-Secretary, noted on 25 November that the chief of the Dublin District Special Branch 'had never felt so optimistic', and believed that 'we are now up against the Gunmen, *not* a nation'. This showed the continuing appeal of the murder gang theory, but in this case it had some factual support. Sturgis added a fortnight later that the arrests were producing a great increase in information, and that the military were 'very cock-a-hoop'.[46]

Optimism was reinforced by other developments. On 28 November in the bloodiest ambush so far, a patrol of Auxiliaries was annihilated at Kilmichael, county Cork. In tactical terms this event was primarily an indictment of the Macroom ADRIC company (which had taken to patrolling on fixed routes), but it also reflected on the effectiveness of the whole 'mobile' policy. The Cabinet recognised this in an oblique way by at last abandoning its resistance to the use of martial law, at least in the south-west. Martial law was proclaimed in Cork on 11 December, and was expected to bring about a speedy rationalisation of policy and unification of command.[47] The army was particularly prone to such expectations. The politicians, however, had not suddenly shed their habitual ambivalence. Sturgis, who himself favoured a temporary military 'dictatorship' to meet the emergency, observed on 14 December that

> The PM's idea, which they (the soldiers) have not grasped, is to have martial law in the distant provinces, as a cloud on the horizon, leaving the seat of government, Dublin, free for them as wants to negotiate – but it's tricky work . . . [48]

The area under martial law was confined in the first instance to four counties, Cork, Kerry, Limerick and Tipperary; it was extended on 30 December to include the whole of General Strickland's 6th Division area, including Clare, Kilkenny, Waterford and Wexford. Even within these eight counties, military control remained limited. The distinctive theoretical feature of martial law, the supersession of the civil legal system by a set of military tribunals responsible only to the military governor, was blurred by the retention of some civil courts. Military tribunals imposed 14 capital sentences during 1921, and in most of these cases appeals were made to the High Court in Dublin, and even to the House of Lords.[49] The higher courts correctly quashed all appeals, on the grounds that a state of war (i.e. rebellion) existed in the south-west and that they could not interfere with the proceedings of military tribunals *durante bello*; but nonetheless, a climate of delay and uncertainty was created which, in Macready's opinion 'nullified the effect of martial law'.[50] The fundamental problem was that the government was still unwilling to admit that outright military measures were needed. Steps regarded as vital by the army, such as a system of controls on entry into Ireland, were refused (though it was Macready himself who opposed Tudor's idea of introducing a system of identity cards within Ireland).

Equally important, unity of command remained a mirage. In February 1921, Macready attempted to secure recognition by the police

forces that Major-General Strickland, General Officer Commanding
(GOC) 6th Division and Military Governor of the Martial Law
Area, was their immediate superior in that area.[51] He gained a
grudging acceptance of this in principle, but in practice the police
retained their independence. The use they made of it was unfortunately illustrated by the fiasco at Castleconnell, county Limerick, in
April, when an Auxiliary raiding party fought a long gun battle
against a group of RIC in a hotel bar, with fatal results to both sides
and to civilians in the middle. A series of killings and lootings in
and near Dublin led to the resignation of the commander of the
Auxiliary division, and to an attempt by Macready to have an
ADRIC company commander court-martialled for murder — an
attempt which was thwarted by Tudor.[52]

It is clear, however, that with all due allowance for the restrictions
under which military measures were conducted, the army itself had
not developed sufficient tactical skills to reap the full benefit of martial
law. Military tribunals, after all, even if left to themselves, could do
nothing until the dangerous rebels were captured. Neither inside nor
outside the Martial Law Area was there any conspicuous success in
this direction. In fact, the surviving evidence suggests that Dublin
District Command was ahead of 6th Division in developing search
techniques. The first big area searches were mounted in Dublin in
January and February: these involved the sealing off of substantial
sectors for a day or more, and they revealed three major technical weaknesses: first, in the troops' capacity to cordon off an area hermetically;
second, in their capacity to make effective searches; and third, in their
capacity to identify wanted men.[53] These weaknesses showed up later
in the rural areas when large-scale 'drives' were attempted. Cordons
proved to be for the most part easily penetrable, searching was often
culpably slack, and the general failure to make the front-line troops
'intelligence-minded' meant that the identification of rebels devolved
upon a handful of specialist officers. These could never cover the
whole of a search area, and without them roundups were well nigh
useless.[54] In view of the persistent paucity of results, it is hard to
resist the conclusion that the army continued these big operations
through inability to think of anything better (and a feeling that, if
nothing else, they were good general training) rather than through
belief in their efficacy.

Certainly the positive results which were achieved in 1921 did not,
in the main, come from big searches. In Dublin, such operations were
soon virtually abandoned, and after a period of frustrating failure it

was the old method of sudden raids, now backed by a better intelligence system, which at last made a significant breakthrough. Between 22 March and 24 April a dramatic series of raids led to the seizure of three machine guns, 16 rifles, 97 revolvers, 305 grenades, and over 10,000 rounds of ammunition.[55] Three days later this haul was doubled at a stroke when an IRA provincial distribution centre was located. Captures on this scale were body blows to the rebels, more so than captures of men, who could usually be replaced. (By the end of April no less than 3,000 rebels had been interned, including 18 brigade commanders and 71 battalion commanders, without noticeable effect on IRA strength.) At the same time, the IRA leadership in Dublin was being put under great pressure, as the increasing number of hair's breadth escapes indicated. Military confidence rose markedly, and played a part in the government's decision not to call a truce for the Irish elections due in mid-May.[56] Of still greater potential significance was a tactical development which was occurring in some rural areas. A belated realisation of the limitations of motor patrols and the futility of big searches led local troops to experiment with small foot columns like those of the IRA, moving freely across country. This was almost the first genuine counter-guerrilla technique to emerge, and the threat it posed was fully recognised by the IRA, whose whole network of communications and safe areas was placed in jeopardy.[57] Yet, apart from an enthusiastic reference to the plan by the RIC County Inspector for North Tipperary, and some evidence that similar small columns were employed in the countryside around Dublin, this idea seems to have been discounted by the higher authorities.[58]

The generals, their later assertions notwithstanding, believed rather in the necessity and efficacy of the scheme of authorised punishments or official reprisals, which Macready had first outlined in September 1920. This became possible after the declaration of martial law, and began at the turn of the year. Public proclamations announced that houses close to the site of ambushes, whose occupants 'were, owing to their proximity to the outrage, or their known political tendencies, implicated in the outrage', would be destroyed.[59] General Strickland declared his faith in this scheme, which 'in spite of the howls of condemnation', he said, 'must have a deterrent effect on those who may be detailed for further outrages'.[60] But beyond such faith there was no concrete evidence of this, to set against the mighty chorus of howls which emanated not only from the dispossessed but also from their irate loyalist landlords. Amidst general opprobrium and Cabinet hostility, the policy was revoked at the beginning of June.[61] Military policy was reduced to the mounting of ever larger-scale searches. 'Drives', as one distinguished military visitor observed, 'seemed to exercise a peculiar fascination over the staff mind, in spite of continual proof that open-country cordons seldom trapped any rebels who were determined to escape'.[62] When Macready drew up, on 23 May, a major Cabinet memorandum on the military situation, he declared that,

> Apart from little expeditions of a couple of subaltern officers and from 12 to 20 men, extending over from 24 to 48 hours, and directed against a spot where information has been received of a collection of rebels, . . . the only possibility of offensive action lies with the Cavalry . . . [63]

If this was true, then the prospects were even bleaker than Macready implied, since between 27 May and 15 June the 5th Division mounted a mammoth series of cavalry drives, employing four cavalry regiments backed up by local troops, and sweeping across eight midland counties. The results, in terms of captures, were insignificant.[64]

Macready's memorandum was not, however, a purely military appreciation. It was his last attempt to force the government to accept what he had always argued — that Britain could not, or would not, pay the moral and physical price of crushing Irish resistance. The memorandum concluded ominously that

> the present state of affairs in Ireland, so far as regards the troops serving there, must be brought to a conclusion by October, or steps must be taken to relieve practically the whole of the troops together with the great majority of the commanders and their staffs.

In other words, the strain had brought the army near to the end of its tether. Throughout the critical period of May and June, when the Irish elections took place, and the Cabinet discussed the possibility of declaring Crown Colony government with full martial law if Sinn Féin refused to participate in the new Southern Parliament, Macready painted the military future in what Balfour called 'the most ensanguined hue', seeking to bring home to the Cabinet that the most intense and violent measures would have to be employed during the summer if further repression were decided upon.[65]

Henry Wilson underwrote Macready's ultimata, though he misunderstood Macready's intention. All along, Wilson had held that the

government should 'get on or get out', and left no one in doubt that
his preference was for the former course. The latter, he believed, would
signal the breakup of the British Empire. He consistently advocated
ruthless coercion, including the reprisal shooting of Sinn Féiners 'by
roster'. The intensity of his feeling was such that Lloyd George complained that one could 'never get a sane discussion with him' about
Ireland.[66] In the end, his ferocity backfired. The sombre military
prognostications, which he hoped would alert the Cabinet to the peril
of defeat, served rather to prepare the ground for negotiation. Although
large military reinforcements were dispatched to Ireland in mid-June,
there was little political will to use them.[67] Lord Birkenhead declared
in the House of Lords on 21 June that 'the history of the last three
months is the history of the failure of our military measures to keep
pace with, and to overcome, the military measures which have been
taken by our opponents'.[68] There could be no sort of guarantee that
the next three months would not tell the same story. For the Cabinet,
with its rooted hostility towards the use of naked military rule
within the United Kingdom, enough was enough.

One of the primary problems in war is, of course, uncertainty about
the situation on the opposite side. Overestimation of an opponent's
strength can be as serious an error as underestimation. Was the military
picture supplied to the Cabinet substantially accurate? No certain
answer can be returned to this, but the surviving evidence does suggest
that Macready overestimated the IRA's resilience. There can be no
doubt that the Republican position was in many respects deteriorating
in 1921. British operational intelligence improved sufficiently to reveal
the serious weaknesses in the IRA's own system. Flying columns, impressive in number, were less so in performance. All but a handful
threshed about impotently, seldom able to locate British forces and
usually too weak to engage them if they did. January and February
were perhaps the nadir for the rural units, but thereafter the momentum of 1920 could not be regained. The defiant creation of divisional
commands in April had no operational effect, and rather served to
underline internal imbalances. Except perhaps in parts of Cork and
Kerry, the IRA offensive had ground to a standstill. Petty operations,
murders, mail raids and robberies multiplied, ambitious actions
declined. Widespread fragmentation of local units occurred. Desertion
began to be a problem, and British drives, though unproductive of
concrete effects, piled on increasing pressure. IRA commanders
expressed the same fears about the strain on their men as did Macready.[69]
In Dublin itself the pressure was especially severe, and produced a

gloomy realism amounting almost to pessimism on the part of leaders like Mulcahy and Collins. [70]

All this did not, however, amount to the sort of British victory that the politicians required. A recent and penetrating study of County Clare in this period has suggested that by 1921 'both sides were virtually impregnable', and that finally 'both sides acknowledged defeat'.[71] While this may exaggerate the nature of the stalemate, it makes a fundamental point. Even if, as seems likely, an intensified British effort in the summer could have substantially altered the military balance (it might well, for instance, have destroyed the flying columns and left the remnant of the organisation in disarray), it could not have eradicated the IRA altogether in 1921, or excised its public support. It did not matter if the IRA survived by the skin of its teeth: the vital thing was survival. In the end, the physical balance was subordinate to the moral balance. The Republic outlasted Britain's will to crush it. The British government had always been faced, though it had refused to recognise it, with the alternatives of extirpating the insurgents or making terms with them. By misreading the seriousness of the insurgency, the Cabinet had contrived to avoid the issue for two years, but two years of messy, directionless violence had effectively eroded its freedom of choice. By mid-1921 to continue the war seemed more unacceptable than to make terms. The 'restoration of order' had failed, partly because of faulty policies, and partly because of the political restrictions imposed upon the military forces. If, as Lloyd George said, the European states-man 'stumbled into war' in 1914, Lloyd George's government did the same in 1919. The Anglo-Irish war was primarily a product of neglect, and it was neglect which governed its halting progress and determined its outcome.

Notes

1. Military intelligence report, Midland and Connaught District, Oct. 1916, Public Record Office, London, CO 904 157.
2. See K.B. Nowlan, 'Dáil Eireann and the Army: Unity and Division', in T.D. Williams (ed.), *The Irish Struggle 1916–1926* (London, 1966), pp. 70–3.
3. I have attempted to deal with this issue in greater depth in 'The Irish Republican Army and the Development of Guerrilla warfare', *English Historical Review* (forthcoming).
4. David Fitzpatrick's study of County Clare, *Politics and Irish Life 1913–1921* (Dublin, 1977), p. 224, suggests that 'The motive for almost every violent engagement can, indeed, be traced to one driving, self-preservative obsession: to get arms, and to use them to get more arms.'
5. Armed, however, not with Lee Enfield rifles but with Martini-Henry

carbines. Although portrayed by its opponents as an army of occupation, its military skills were virtually non-existent, as was to be repeatedly demonstrated. Even the use of barbed wire baffled them – see, e.g., Head Constable Eagar, RIC Kenmare, to O.C. Troops Berehaven, Co. Cork, 22 April 1920, National Library of Ireland, Pos. 918.

6.   See outrage statistics in Charles Townshend, *The British Campaign in Ireland 1919–1921* (Oxford, 1975), App. V, p. 214.

7.   The politically more explicit title 'Irish Republican Army' came into extensive use in 1919, but a fair number of Volunteer units never adopted it. The organisation remained officially *Oglaigh na hEireann*.

8.   See Fitzpatrick, *Politics and Irish Life 1913–1921*, Ch. 6.

9.   Tom Jones (ed. K. Middlemas), *Whitehall Diary* (London, 1971), vol. III, p. 17.

10.   French to Macpherson, 20 Oct. 1919, Strathcarron MSS Bodleian Library, Oxford; Cabinet Conference, 14 Nov. 1919 PRO, C. 8 (19) App. IV, CAB 23 18.

11.   The imminence of collapse has been stressed by many writers, but they never specify what is meant by this. What in fact happened was that resignations ran higher than intake for several months, but never neared the epidemic proportions entailed in the concept of 'collapse'. The resilience of the force surprised all observers, including its own commanders.

12.   Report of Sir Warren Fisher, 12 May, in Bonar Law to Lloyd Geroge, 13 May 1920, House of Lords, Lloyd George MSS, F/31/1/32.

13.   Approximately 1,200 strong, confined to Dublin, from which (until the appearance of the Auxiliaries) the RIC was excluded.

14.   GOC-in-Chief Ireland to Lord Lieutenant, 23 Apr. 1920, House of Lords, Bonar Law MSS, 103/2/16. Macready's post between the end of the Great War and April 1920 was Commissioner of the London Metropolitan Police. Macready insisted upon an unprecedented disturbance allowance of £5000 for going to Ireland, provoking the Secretary of State for War (Winston Churchill) to protest, 'We shall hear next of a General Officer stipulating for forty or fifty thousand pounds in order to undertake a particularly difficult or hazardous campaign'. Note to Chancellor of the Exchequer, 4 Apr. 1920, PRO, W.O. 32 4815.

15.   GOC-in-Chief to Under Secretary, 28 May 1920, Anderson MSS, PRO, C.O. 904 188; Sir C.F.N. Macready, *Annals of an Active Life* (London, 1924), vol. II, p. 459. Tudor's initial title was the rather nebulous 'Police Adviser'; the less ambiguous 'Chief of Police' emerged later.

16.   Cabinet Conference, 23 July 1920, PRO, CP 1693, CAB 24 109.

17.   For considered military verdicts on the ADRIC, see GOC 6th Div. to GOC-in-Chief Ireland, 3 Jan. 1921, PRO, WO 35 88(1); Macready to Frances Stevenson, 20 June 1921, Lloyd George MSS, F/36/3/19. Tudor admitted to the Cabinet in December that 'Drink was the problem' with the Auxiliaries.

18.   Inspector General (Brigadier-General Byrne) to Under Secretary, 4 Oct. 1919, Strathcarron MSS.

19.   Cabinet Conference, 23 July 1920, PRO, CP 1693, CAB 24 109, and Jones, *Whitehall Diary*, vol. III, pp. 25–7.

20.   GHQ Irish Command, *Record of the Rebellion in Ireland* (1922) App. III, Imperial War Museum (IWM), Jeudwine MSS, 73/82/2. See Mark Sturgis' diary, 14 Aug. 1920, PRO, 30 59/1.

21.   Jones, *Whitehall Diary*, 15 Feb. 1921, vol. III, p. 52; on the *Weekly Summary* see General Gough's article 'The Situation in Ireland' in *Review of Reviews*, LXIII, Feb. 1921, p. 35.

22.   GHQ Irish Command, *Record of the Rebellion in Ireland*, vol. I, p. 5.

23.   GHQ (1) to Dublin District, 21 Jan. 1920, D.D. HQ File, PRO, W.O. 35 70.

24. Fisher's report, Appendix, Lloyd George MSS, F/31/1/32.
25. GHQ Irish Command, vol. II, pp. 4–5, 21, 23–4; IQM. Percival MSS, Lecture 2, p. 6.
26. GHQ Irish Command, *Record of the Rebellion in Ireland*, vol. I, p. 77; Greenwood to Bonar Law, 16 May 1920. Bonar Law MSS, 103/3/9.
27. Macready to Long, 23 Apr., and to Lloyd George, 1 May 1920. Lloyd George MSS. F/34/1/19 and F/36/2/13.
28. 'History of the 5th Division in Ireland, 1919–1922', pp. 30–1. IWM. Jeudwine MSS, 72/82/2.
29. Note of conversation, 30 Apr. 1920, PRO, CAB. 23 20; Hankey's diary, 23 May 1920 (communication from Capt. S.J. Roskill).
30. GHQ Irish Command, *Record of the Rebellion in Ireland*, vol. I, p. 5; Hist. 5th Div., p. 9; *General Annual Report on the British Army, 1919–20*, Cmd. 1610 xii 611 (1922), p. 10.
31. GOC-in-Chief Ireland, Weekly situation report (WSR), 8 Jan. 1921, PRO, C.P. 2456, CAB 24 118.
32. Weekly totals (occasionally erratic) in Chief Secretary's Weekly Surveys, for 1920 (CAB 27 108) and 1921 (CAB 24 118ff.). ADRIC Register no. 1, PRO H.O. 184 50.
33. GOC-in-Chief to Chief Secretary, 17 July 1920. Lloyd George MSS, F/19/2/12.
34. GOC 5th Div. to GOC-in-Chief, 23 July 1920. IWM. Jeudwine MSS, 72/82/2. The railway embargo began in May and continued until mid-December.
35. Tudor had reminded the Cabinet on 23 July that so far not a single murderer had been brought to justice. PRO, C.P. 1693, CAB 24 109.
36. Dublin Castle statements, Oct. 1920, PRO, C.O. 904 168/1.
37. GOC-in-Chief Ireland to CIGS, 28 Sept. 1920, PRO, Anderson MSS, C.O. 904,188/1.
38. Townshend, *The British Campaign in Ireland 1919–1921*, p. 120.
39. Bonar Law MSS, 103/3/26.
40. GOC-in-Chief WSR, 27 Aug. 1920. Irish Situation Committee (SIC) 32, PRO, CAB 27 108.
41. General Staff 6th Div. to Brigades, 6 (?) July 1920. Captured document in Department of Defence Archives: Collins MSS, NLI Pos. 918.
42. F.E. Kitson, *Low Intensity Operations* (London, 1971), Ch. 6.
43. GHQ Irish Command, *Record of the Rebellion in Ireland*, vol. II, pp. 30, 33.
44. The apologia in his autobiography *Winter's Tale* (London, 1955) should be counterbalanced by the opinions of his critics. See Townshend, *British Campaign*, pp. 126–7, 169, 204.
45. DD War Diary, 23 Nov. 1920, PRO, W.O. 35 90/1; Under Secretary to Chief Secretary, 21 Nov. 1920, PRO, Anderson MSS, C.O. 904 188/1; GOC-in-Chief WSR, 27 Nov. 1920, PRO, SIC 59, CAB 27 108.
46. Sturgis' diary, 25 Nov. and 9 Dec. 1920, PRO 30 59/3.
47. On 10 Dec., 6th Div. orders stated that 'It is essential that very close touch should be kept between Military Governors and their subordinate Commanders, and the Heads of the various Police Forces in their Area, so that the full benefit may be derived from Unity of Command. Military Governors should feel themselves responsible for the operations in their Area of all Forces of |the Crown . . . the highest standard of discipline is essential . . . The practice by which commanders appear in certain cases to turn to wilfully blind eye to the misdoings of those under their Command, must cease immediately.' NLI, Collins MSS, Pos. 918.
48. Sturgis' diary, 14 Dec. 1920. For his ideas on military 'dictatorship' see

entries for 17, 19, 24 Aug., 20 Sept. 1920; 23, 28 Feb. 1921, PRO 30 59/1–4.

49. R.V. Murphy, R.V. Allen, R. (Garde) v. Strickland, R. (Ronayne and Mulcahy) v. Strickland, Jan.–Apr. 1921, 2 IR 190, 241, 317, 328, 333.

50. Macready, *Annals of an Active Life*, vol. II, p. 517.

51. GOC-in-Chief to Under Secretary, 14 Feb. 1921, Anderson MSS, CO 904 188/2.

52. Townshend, *British Campaign*, pp. 163–5, 166–8.

53. Reports of 24th and 25th Provisional Brigade conferences, 21 Jan. 1921, DD HQ File, PRO, WO 35 71.

54. Remarks by OC Kerry Brigade, 6th Div. orders 6 July 1921, PRO, WO 35 71.

55. DD HQ File.

56. Jones, *Whitehall Diary*, vol. III, p. 70.

57. F. O'Donoghue, *No Other Law* (Dublin, 1954), pp. 166–7.

58. RIC Reports, May 1921, CO 904 115; Orders for 26th Provisional Brigade, June 1921, WO 35 93(1)4.

59. GOC-in-Chief WSR, 1 Jan. 1921, SIC 68, CAB 27 108.

60. GOC 6th Div. to GOC-in-Chief, 22 Jan. 1921, WO 35 88(1).

61. Cabinet minutes, 2 June 1921, C 47(21), CAB 23 25.

62. Memo. by Sir High Elles, OC Tank Corps Centre, circulated to Cabinet by Secretary of State for War, 24 June 1921, CP 3075, CAB 24 124.

63. Memo. 'A', GOC-in-Chief Ireland to Cabinet, 23 May 1921, CP 2965 CAB 24 123.

64. Hist. 5th Div., p. 97 and App. XVII, IWM 72/82/2.

65. Cabinet Irish Situation Committee, 26 May, 15 June 1921, SIC 8th Conclusions, CAB 27 107; Jones, *Whitehall Diary*, vol. III, pp. 76–7.

66. Cabinet, 2 June 1921, Jones, *Whitehall Diary*, vol. II, pp. 76–7.

67. In fact the strength of Irish Command had actually declined during 1921 owing to drafts overseas and calls from battalions to cross to Britain to counter industrial unrest, but 17 extra battalions arrived between 14 June and 7 July.

68. 45 HL Deb. 5s, col. 690.

69. GHQ Staff memo., 30 Mar. 1921; no. 1 Bde., 1st Northern Div. to Chief of Staff, 22 May 1921; UCD, Mulcahy MSS, P7/A/II/17, 19.

70. Their later arguments in favour of the Treaty were based on the belief that the IRA had reached, if not passed, its military limit.

71. Fitzpatrick, *Politics and Irish Life*, pp. 225, 230.

4 THE MALAYAN EMERGENCY

Anthony Short

A rather dated assertion from the book *Guerrillas in the Sixties* reads:

> Basically, the problem is a political one; to attempt to understand
> it in purely military terms is the most dangerous kind of over-
> simplification. Guerrillas are a symptom rather than a cause. Lasting
> success requires a viable political settlement, and even operational
> success over a period of time demands a proper political frame-
> work for effective military action.[1]

If this is true, then it will be most important to look at the Malayan
political problem as a whole (of which the insurgency is a part). In
this regard 'political' is defined here as a power relationship not only
within a society but, as this was a colonial society, between it and the
government which had been created on its behalf, which had been
superseded in the course of the greatest imperial defeat suffered by
Britain (setting aside some untoward events with the thirteen colonies)
and, in 1945, which was on the point of being restored by force of
arms to a country still occupied by the Japanese.

With the exception of Burma and the Philippines it is now
becoming more and more obvious that wartime arrangements, a
dearth of intelligence, and some remarkable clandestine activities –
not to speak of the effects of Japanese occupation – created an entirely
new set of conditions and problems by the time the colonial powers,
and more especially France and the Netherlands, returned to South-East
Asia in 1945. In Malaya, it is important to remember that what intelligence was gathered of the wartime situation mostly came in a rush in
the concluding months of the war when, with Burmese bases available,
and with the introduction of longer range aircraft, it was possible for
the first time to cover the entire length of the Malayan peninsula and
to drop agents, wireless teams and support groups who were then able
to make contact with the local guerrillas. As for the guerrillas themselves,
the fact of Malayan Chinese resistance in the form of the Malayan
Peoples Anti-Japanese Army (MPAJA) is comparatively well known.
But this resistance was complicated by the presence (as in occupied
Western and parts of Eastern Europe) of anti-communist guerrillas (in

this case, the Kuomintang-supporting Chinese); and the perhaps lesser
known fact of Malay resistance units (of which the late Malaysian Prime
Minister, Tun Razak, was a member) which upsets the fairly common
assumption that, on the whole, the Chinese resisted and the Malays
'collaborated'.

Those who seek also a general pattern of colonial struggle in South-
East Asia after the war usually have to concentrate on Singapore in
order to find the turbulent events which may be thought to approximate to Chinese resistance in Malaya to a returning colonial power; but
in Malaya itself the re-establishment of colonial rule is something
which too often seems to be taken for granted. Here and elsewhere in
South-East Asia there was a critical interregnum between the Japanese
surrender and the return of imperial forces; and although there was not
even an approach in Malaya to the independence sponsored by the
Japanese in Indonesia or declared by Ho Chi Minh in Tonking, there
were obvious but seldom recorded opportunities for guerrilla units of
the Chinese Resistance to 'liberate' remote villages and small towns and
to claim, both then and afterwards, that this was done by their own
force of arms. There was also a dark side to the end of Japanese
occupation. In part associated with the reprisals taken by guerrillas on
actual or suspected collaborators, but at times apparently spontaneous,
there were outbreaks of intercommunal slaughter of Malays and Chinese
which, until well into the period of British Military Administration,
required special summaries and constant attention.

In the period between August 1945 and June 1948 what is perhaps
most consistently underestimated is the extent to which 'government'
had *not* been re-established in Malaya. There is perhaps a tendency to
concentrate, on the formal level, on the fortunes and misfortunes of
proposed political structures. While it may be said that the Malayan
Union failed and the Federation of Malaya succeeded, these were
developments which primarily concerned the badly shaken Malay
community. However, they were also events where observers did not
take into account the influence of Malay-Indonesian radicalism. This
small but important element was something which absorbed too much of
the attention of the under-manned, post-war Malayan Security Services.
Even where the radical movement is very competently dealt with, as in
Means' *Malaysian Politics*,[2] it is again Malay radicalism, and still comparatively little is known of the politics of the dislocated Malayan
Chinese community.

Here, it would seem that a different time scale would help to
establish certain important features of the political potential of the

Malayan Chinese although, again, one should look at radical Chinese
politics in both its institutional and unorganised forms. Before the war,
for example, one would need to pick out the importance of the policy
change in the Malayan Communist Party in which, after the Japanese
invasion of China, comparatively sterile appeals to a largely non-existent
proletariat were succeeded by the simple and successful appeal to
Chinese patriotism. At about the same time, although again most im-
perfectly recorded, there would seem to have been a strong and
important 'Robin Hood' component (and not simply rather romantic
notions of Chinese banditry) in those who escaped from the virtual
latifundia of Chinese estates and concessions in Johore — which, for
government purposes, were reckoned to be beyond the pale — and lived,
literally, as outlaws.

The attempt of some hundreds of thousands of Chinese to move, in
effect, beyond the pale of Japanese administration during the war is,
again, comparatively well known although, once more, the significance
of the sheer number of rural Chinese who remained outside the limits
of government activity and knowledge has not always been grasped. On
a more settled level — of cities, towns and large villages — the decision
to scrap the pre-war Chinese Protectorate, now regarded at best as an
anachronism, may be taken as evidence of a subsequent failure of
government intelligence as to what was happening within the Chinese
community. For several hundred thousand Chinese squatters the alternative to a remote, uncovenanted and rather unacceptable government
lay in the essential anti-government of more or less improvised peasant
resistance.

However, for the Malayan Communist Party (MCP) the most
spectacular gains were made after the war, not in the development of
peasant communism, but in the creation and maintenance of a strong-
hold in the trade unions. The ability to paralyse the Singapore docks
was a spectacular and impressive demonstration of power while the
close liaison and in some cases interchangeable leadership between the
local unions and MCP branches, as well as higher-level correlation
between the Federations of Trade Unions (FTU) and the Party, ensured
an integrated political and economic struggle. Apart from the larger
towns, where it is tempting to believe that the MCP/FTU leadership
found life more congenial, there were also the possibilities of exploring
the political potential of Indian estate labour. Already to a certain
extent radicalised during the war, and with the independence of India
soon to be an accomplished fact, a volatile situation existed on a
number of estates as situations of near and actual riot bear out.

Whether this could be capitalised by Indian and occasional Tamil-speaking Chinese members of the MCP, and whether Indian estate labour could, in effect, be detached from the area of government control, was an issue that was hardly decided until the actual state of emergency was declared; and while it is probably an exaggeration to say that some estates, particularly Chinese-owned, from which the managers had prudently retired, formed part of an irregular pattern of rural *soviets*, nevertheless in their half-formed plans and the perhaps only half-understood possibilities of bringing down colonial and capitalist enterprise in Malaya, Indian, and to a lesser extent, Chinese labour on particular rubber estates provided an approximate vanguard to a rural proletariat.

Certain similarities with pre-revolutionary Cuba suggest themselves, both on the plantations and in the unions, but in neither country could it be said that a rural proletariat was the same thing as a peasantry.[3] In Malaya the organisation of estate labour seemed to offer a better return to the MCP until the 'armed struggle' began than any comparable work with Chinese peasantry — the Malay peasantry at this time being largely ignored. But it could be argued that their neglect of Chinese peasant farmers had significantly reduced the Party's chances of success once the insurrection had begun. For all that they sought to follow the Chinese revolutionary model, the experiences of the Malayan Chinese had been very different and there had been nothing like the long process of preparation, as in the Yenan period, when 'the penetration of the natural village' had laid the foundation for the eventual success of the Chinese Communist Party. Of course both geography and history had been different in Malaya but the MCP did not, in the pre-insurrectionary period, strive to identify themselves with the scattered Chinese squatters, nor was there any obvious correlation between the two.

In any event it may be argued that there was hardly any sufficient cause for revolution in Malaya in 1948: at least not one that would provide leaders with adequate support. As far as the Malayan Chinese peasantry was concerned, there was really no comparison, for example, with the hardships they would have experienced in China. Malaya as a whole, like most of South-East Asia, had suffered considerably during the war and its aftermath, but while the process of economic and social reconstruction took its time, things were getting better, not worse — although, as de Tocqueville pointed out, a revolution might be expected at just such a time. Gamba and Stenson, in their work on trade unions in Malaya and Singapore and the origins of the insurrection, both suggest that it was a more or less self-igniting revolution.[4] For Stenson, it was a case of 'moderation' on one side and aggressive restriction on the other to the point where the leaders of the Pan Malayan Federation of Trade Unions were, as he puts it, left 'with no alternative'. This suggests that instead of continuing as individual unions, the leaders had to take to the jungle, there to continue the struggle, as Clausewitz might have put it, with a mixture of other means.

Overall, Stenson prefers to discount the offensive intentions of the MCP in 1948 and, in particular, questions the existence of an insurrectionary programme. Their recognition, however, that 'open armed conflict was likely to occur during the course of 1948 or possibly 1949' begs the question 'how', although in respect of the day-to-day origins of the armed struggle there is certainly a sense in which both sides stumbled into action against each other. The simple thesis that instructions came from Moscow via the Calcutta conferences — both the World Federation of Democratic Youth and the Second Congress of the Communist Party of India (CPI) — to the communist parties of South-East Asia is rightly discounted (it is surprising the extent to which it is still an accredited myth). It makes much more sense to see the Malayan insurrection in its proper local context. Revolutionary enthusiasm was undoubtedly there — it is interesting and ironical to note that at the CPI congress in Calcutta the 'forward line' was taken by the Yugoslavs with the Russians holding back — and in the end, the MCP took its critical decisions regarding the armed struggle at its fourth and fifth Plenary meetings in March and May 1948. By mid-June, after the hard-core MCP members had already taken to the jungle, any other Party supporters still in doubt were told categorically in the *Min Sheng Pao*: 'All in all, for the sake of our lives, we cannot procrastinate any more nor can we give in any further but we must fight our way out through struggle.'

Elsewhere in South-East Asia — Vietnam, say, in December 1946 or Indonesia at the time of either the first or second Dutch 'police actions' — one might be disposed to take such an argument on the part of nationalists at its face value. After all, throughout the area, colonial rule had been destroyed by the Japanese and the appearance of embattled or demonstrative nationalist movements at least confronted with a rival claim to legitimacy the colonial power which seemed to some to be returning like the Bourbons in the baggage train of their principal ally. At the same time, it also seemed to others that the Japanese wartime occupation had, in some way, like losing the mandate of heaven, destroyed that colonial legitimacy once and for all. Was

Malaya exceptional and if so, in what respect? As a matter of imminent fact it might be argued that Malaya was about to be wrested from Japanese control by force of British arms and that, had this happened, this manifest demonstration of British power and, in a sense, vindication of their protection of the Malay States, would have retrieved the political situation and the course of history would have been different. In the event this did not happen and after a half-hearted experiment with the Malayan Union, the *status quo ante bellum* was restored. In this situation, perhaps, one should think of the Malayan Communist Party as a genuine vanguard, not only of the proletariat, but of all the progressive forces in Malaya who sought to hasten the millennium not only by putting an end to colonial rule but also by ensuring that, when independence came, it came on terms that would not permit the establishment of neo-colonialism. To do this, however, one must take the MCP at its own valuation: as the repository and best judge of the people's interests and as the executive of the popular will. One must also, somehow, square the circle so that the largely Chinese, and Chinese-directed party apparatus, not to mention those who fought and died in the insurgent cause, was representative not only of the alienated segment of Malayan Chinese society, but of the predominant Malay community as well. Once the insurrection had begun, the MCP did achieve some short-lived success in the Malay riverine *kampongs* of Pahang and in 1955 a Malay appeared as one of the party triumvirate at the Baling peace talks, while in more recent years, and in spite of temptations to be contrary, the party has stressed the supracommunal aspect of its cause. Overall, however, there can be no doubt that this was a Chinese insurrection: nominally Malayan Chinese but with considerable numbers of the China-born whose principal allegiance must be reckoned to have been to China rather than to Malaya.

In terms of modern revolutionary theory on the recourse to political violence, the insurrection in Malaya offers material to support the conclusions of at least one recent book on rebellions.[5] In another,[6] each of the four main characteristics noted — economic causes, the failure of society to meet demands put upon it, the individual's sense of alienation from society and the simple displacement of political power — may also be seen in Malaya in 1948; and to these might well be added a situation in which the structure of government, while it did not embody the representative principle and while it was proceeding on no announced or fixed timetable for its own liquidation, nevertheless represented the realities — although perhaps in Malaya its critics would call it the artifices — of political power that had certainly existed in 1939. A hundred years earlier, Lord Durham had found in Canada two nations at war in the bosom of a single state, and a system of irresponsible government; and while it could hardly be said that in Malaya the two principal communities, Malay and Chinese, were at war in 1948, nevertheless, almost as soon as the insurrection began, the country seemed to be divided, if not polarised, into those who, such as hastily recruited Malay special constables, were actively supporting the government and those, in particular the Chinese insurgents, who were against it.

At the outset the overall failure of the intelligence either to forecast the form and timing of the insurrection, or to provide anything like an enemy order of battle once it had started, seemed to give the insurgents important advantages although these, for the most part, were not taken. Had anything like full insurgent mobilisation been possible before co-ordinated guerrilla attacks began — and had they remembered or been able to use the tactics which, on the eve of the scheduled Allied invasion of 1945, had convinced Spencer Chapman[7] at least that they would have been a formidable force — then it is possible that they could have achieved such economic and perhaps social and political dis-location as would, by its very success, have attracted the active support that they needed in the opening phase. As it was, there were large numbers of incidents such as frequent murders of their political opponents among Kuomintang supporters. However, there were few pitch-ed battles; nor was there the occupation of more than one or two villages for a few days or hours, and there was little to provide the momentum that might have overwhelmed parts of the country. Nevertheless, for small patrols of police and soldiers in a largely unfamiliar situation, the dangers and frustrations of dealing with suspect, sullen or hostile Chinese villagers and peasant farmers sometimes spilled over into acts of violence, retribution and meanness to the point where, in the latter part of 1948, there was something that approximated to the beginning of a counter-terror; or so it might have seemed to Malayan Chinese.

Up to this point, however, government, while it may have been badly informed and lacking in decisiveness, had acted with commend-able restraint. The High Commissioner, Sir Edward Gent, and the Commissioner of Police had both been withdrawn and critical decisions were taken by the Commissioner General in South-East Asia, Mr Malcolm MacDonald. Among them was that which identified the importance of the rubber estates and their defence, for which, as mentioned, large numbers of Malay special constables were recruited. As important was the decision that wherever possible government should continue very much as usual and, although in the worst phases of the campaign some police stations were closed and significantly large areas of country were at least dominated by the guerrillas, most of the time there was an astonishing air of normality to Malaya during the Emergency – at least in the towns and most of the villages. In the remote rural areas, however, where most of the Chinese peasant farmers and smallholders existed as squatters on land to which they were not legally entitled, but to whose existence government had generally turned a blind eye, it was assumed that guerrillas had a free run. At first, three possibilities of dealing with them were suggested: that they should be detained, deported or dispersed. But with no over-all plan, unresolved disputes as to whether it was a federal or a state matter, and little sense of urgency, it is not surprising that by the time the guerrillas renewed their assault in 1950, almost nothing had been achieved other than a growing sense of bitterness and alienation among many, if not most, rural Chinese.

Although the insurgents themselves had achieved little in the opening months of the Emergency, and had then seemed to melt away into the jungle, their offensive potential was never seriously impaired in 1949 and, more important, as the High Commissioner, Sir Henry Gurney, reported in January 1950: 'The political brains behind the Communist efforts remain for practical purposes untouched and un-located.' Six months later, when the Korean war began, the tide of Asian communism, which had already been seen to turn in China, now seemed to be coming in fast and lapping at the Western positions which remained in Asia. In Malaya, while the renewed guerrilla assault obviously depended in part upon their successful retraining and re-grouping, it also depended on the at least tacit support of large numbers of Chinese and, at this point, there was little incentive for them to declare their allegiance either to the existing colonial government or to a future, independent Malaya, whose shape was yet unknown. In the meantime, with Asian communism, backed by the power of China, seen to be the wave of the future, it was an understandable tendency for Malayan Chinese to hedge their bets which, in turn, contributed to the exasperation of both the colonial government and the Malay community. At this time it is important to remember the comparative strength of the guerrilla organisation. Not only were they almost equal to Security Forces in the matter of supplies and superior in intelligence gathering, but recruitment was more than keeping pace with their casualties. A new GOC had already asked for another brigade, that being, as he put it, 'the only means of giving the breathing space required by the civil and police authority to put in hand the decisive measures that they alone can take' but at the end of 1950 all that could be said was that the civil measures had not failed and that they gave some hope of success in the future.

For this hope of success to become a reality, there were two essential requirements. First, that government forces should be working to an effective overall plan, and second, that government had to find a way of securing the allegiance of substantial numbers of Malayan Chinese which meant, of course, that confidence in the support of the guerrillas would be conversely that much reduced. The appointment of a retired lieutenant general, Sir Harold Briggs, as first Director of Operations brought with it what may be regarded as the essential master plan in which the security forces would now aim to eliminate both the armed guerrillas and the *Min Yuen*, their support organisation: a notable advance as, until then, the army had too often been in search of battalion-sized targets and decisive battles. The plan itself was to be executed by a small Federal War Council plus State and Settlement War Executive Committees. The first big 'drive' of the Briggs Plan in Johore in June 1950 was, however, largely a failure: on the analogy of the mosquito, some were killed but the breeding grounds were largely untouched. A year later, however, when Gurney and Briggs informed the Colonial Office that they had reached the turning point of the campaign this was true, and almost prophetic, but government, at this time, seemed to have run out of steam and, at all events, lacked the impetus to carry its burden over the crest of the hill and thus begin the more comfortable descent to ultimate victory. In particular, the police were suffering from internal controversies, their para-military functions were emphasised to the exclusion of almost every-thing else, and the essential resettlement was being held up because of a shortage of police posts. In one state, Perak, the special con-stabulary were described as being no longer an effective force, which, perhaps, when one considers that the Commissioner of Police in Malaya was responsible for more men, including special constables, than there were in the rest of the Colonial Police Service put together, should not have been altogether surprising. Little effective resettlement or re-grouping of estate labour had been done in 1950 or 1951 at a time when the campaign may be said to have reached its climax, and in the battle for the New Villages, particularly in the second half of 1951, it was obvious that Gurney himself had begun to lose confidence in the Malayan Chinese. Then, almost at a stroke, the principals of govern-ment were removed. Gurney, the High Commissioner, was ambushed and killed. Gray, the Commissioner of Police, and Jenkin, the Director of Intelligence, were both removed. Briggs, the Director of Operations, retired after only eighteen months and died shortly after.

The immediate aftermath of Gurney's death was a wave of recrimination against the Chinese and it was in these circumstances the more remarkable when the new Colonial Secretary, Oliver Lyttelton, visited Malaya, that he should have insisted on racial unity as a prerequisite for independence. When Gurney's replacement, General, later Field-Marshal, Sir Gerald Templer, arrived it was equally remarkable, at least in retrospect, that his principal impact on the course of events was political rather than military. Templer argued that there were three priorities to be followed: first, a sound police force, second, improved intelligence organisation, and third, what he called telling the people the truth. Apart from the galvanic energy which he supplied, Templer's administration was distinguished by the introduction of local elections, councils for the Chinese New Villages (ex-squatter areas) which were an enormous advance in Chinese citizenship and the first openings for Chinese in the Malayan Civil Service. His Commissioner of Police, Colonel Arthur Young from the City of London, also projected a civilian image, halved the numbers in the police, and sought to turn his para-military forces into something that was rather closer to the style of an old-fashioned London bobby. Militarily, it was now recognised that speculative army patrolling and ambushes, and the generally unsuccessful big operations, were no substitute for good intelligence where the surrendered guerrilla provided the best possible source. How to get him to surrender was now something that required a completely integrated civil/military operation for, like the Security Forces, the guerrillas had already decided that they had no future on their own in the deep jungle. The MCP itself had run into serious ideological difficulties and the October Directives of 1951 — ironically the month in which they succeeded in killing the High Commissioner — were a recognition that, if they had not failed, they had at least been premature in launching the armed struggle and that the key to their victory lay in a political reactivation of the masses. This, then, was to be the new battleground and it was here, from the government point of view, that success could only be won by a combination of pressure and engendered confidence among the rural Malayan Chinese. To make it worthwhile for the Chinese to take risks was the fundamental and long-term problem facing the Federal government in framing its Chinese policy. In the meantime, the short-term problem was to make it too costly for the Chinese to avoid taking risks. But in the last analysis the solution to both problems was the same: confidence. Without it little intelligence would be forth-coming and although the apparatus for collecting information might be perfected, for example, by the recruitment and training of a sufficient number of Chinese detectives and seconded British Special Branch Officers, it could not take advantage of what was not there.

Ultimately, therefore, one might argue that it was this intangible quality that created the conditions for the defeat of the communist Chinese insurrection. When Chinese Home Guard sections were fully armed and entirely in control of the defence of their own New Villages, or when Commonwealth soldiers, in the mortal peril of ambush situations, were prepared to let the first shot be fired and the trap be sprung by the accompanying surrendered guerrilla, these must obviously rate as expressions of confidence. On the other hand, when one remembers that no attempt was made to use the thousands of weapons in the hands of Malay Home Guards, Special Constables, police and soldiers for anything like a 'final solution' to the Chinese problem, this must also be seen as confidence; and when the Chinese, whether as Home Guards, political leaders, detectives or as a source of information, took their lives into their hands by supporting government, this too represented confidence.

Mutual confidence, however, particularly between the Malay and the Chinese communities was something which, at the beginning of the insurrection, manifestly did not obtain. It would almost certainly not have been possible for Britain, acting as a colonial government, to have resisted a more or less united demand for independence, as there was, say, in Burma or perhaps Indonesia, but at the outset neither the colonial government nor Malay political leaders were in much of a hurry for independence while the radical and militant wings of both Malay and Malayan Chinese nationalism were enthralled to alien powers, the one to Indonesia, the other to China. Where these provided an alternative enthusiasm, the more moderate bulk of both nationalist forces lacked the confidence which, had it been turned against the colonial government, would have made it the victorious ally of the communist guerrillas. Malay nationalism was mobilised in the United Malay National Organisation by Dato Onn and although it continued and flourished after Onn had left, there was little sense of urgency. Neither the Malay nor the Chinese communities could be certain on what terms independence would come. Each feared the preponderance of the other and made the implicit assumption that, in a fairly evenly balanced society, the extremist elements would triumph in both groups.

Put more briefly, there was little prospect at that time that an independent Malaya would emerge as a politically viable state.[8] In both cases
the temptations were there — and were largely avoided. For the Malay,
the existence of the Malayan Chinese in large numbers without obvious
allegiance to Malaya and perhaps likely to succumb to the attractions of
a resurgent China, was problem enough. When to this was added the
apparent volte-face of government who, instead of removing the sources
of disaffection, decided instead on a form of accelerated development in
the Chinese New Villages, to the apparent neglect of the Malay
kampongs, the question might occur to the Malay whether there was
that much advantage in being a supporter of government rather than its
opponent.

Presumably the Chinese New Villages will be, if they are not already,
a subject for the study of development politics. Their achievements at
the time lay not only in ensuring thirty-year grants as a provision of
security of tenure for former squatters, but also in their introduction,
through elected councils, to the political processes which had hitherto
been largely alien to them. Towards the end of the Emergency four
hundred Chinese operational Home Guard sections were entirely
responsible for the defence of New Villages; and it must also be
remembered that the Chinese Liaison Officers were, in many cases,
doing practically the same job as District Officers elsewhere.

It was the approaches to the New Villages that in fact became the
killing ground in the critical phase of the campaign. Guerrillas in the
jungle cannot exist indefinitely on the resources they find there and
they moved, inevitably, to their sources of supply in Chinese New
Villages. Small quantities of supplies thrown over the wire on a pre-
arranged plan would make the visit worthwhile but the more normal
method was to contact the individual tapper or smallholder during the
day and persuade or coerce him to smuggle supplies on a future
occasion. Such suppliers ultimately became the weak link in the
chain but usually only after quite extraordinarily intensive effort on
the part of Security Forces. The denial of food — at once simple and
impossible — was the weapon that was used to destroy the main force
guerrillas, although at times it required a ratio of up to 50 to 1 in the
Security Forces' favour. It could take up to six months, or even more,
before food denial methods and the intelligence buildup gave the army
or police a reasonable chance of successful ambush: that at a certain
place on a certain day, a certain number of men were likely to appear.
Experience eventually showed that no more than two food denial
operations could be attempted at any one time in any one state, and

this would seem to suggest an almost Montgomery-type thoroughness of preparation and something that could have been thrown out of gear had the guerrillas been able to mount some diversionary attacks. As it was, the guerrillas by this time lacked not only momentum but mass and so were unable to upset the comparatively delicate mechanism on which counter-insurgency depended.

In the last phase of the insurrection, when some of the guerrilla groups had merged more or less successfully with the aborigines of the deep jungle, it was a question of winning over their new supporters by such devices as jungle forts and the raising of the remarkable *Senoi Pra'aq* which itself consisted of aborigines and therefore constituted a long-range jungle group such as even the Special Air Service (SAS) had not been able to match. The year of the great surrenders was 1957: spectacular exploits that had led to the contacting of guerrilla formations, usually by surrendered guerrillas, and persuading them to surrender, a process which had remarkable snowball effects. However, two years earlier the first stage of an orderly transition to independence had already been reached, and it was at the end of this year that the Malayan Communist Party sought an opportunity to discuss a negotiated peace with the elected representatives of Malaya and Singapore who were on the brink of independence. Whether the MCP had really hoped that it would be possible for them to cease fighting and resume 'normal' political activities is perhaps something that will never be known. But the temptations for government to begin independence with a clean slate — at least without the burden and the uncertainties of a continuing guerrilla war — must have been enormous, although in the event, the decision that surrender meant surrender — while it entailed rehabilitation or assisted repatriation for those wishing to return to China — was a gamble that allowed an independent Malaya to finish off the jungle war within three years and declare an end to the state of emergency in 1960.

I have suggested elsewhere that the insurrection in Malaya is best considered as a unique event, at least in the pattern of revolutionary war since 1945. In accounting for its failure perhaps the first thing to be remembered is that there was no substantial assistance, at any time, from any point of the compass, and certainly nothing that was comparable to Vietnam, Greece or Algeria. Therefore the insurgents were forced to be self-sufficient. The next point is that, in an ethnically divided community, the guerrilla appeal and support came mainly from less than a half of the population. Some of it, from the Chinese, was more or less spontaneous. Much of it was induced. The Government, on

the other hand, received massive assistance from a substantial propor-
tion of the Malay community. Ultimately, however, this was not
enough. The vast, often underrated, and denigrated success of the New
Villages can hardly be overestimated. Not only as a minor triumph of
almost instant modernisation, but also as a strategic success. Five
hundred New Villages, some five hundred thousand people, meant that
the principal, indeed almost the only, source of guerrilla supplies was
practically denied to them. The third point concerns the balance of
forces. While the ratio was at times too low to allow the dominance of
the Security Forces, the guerrillas never achieved that critical mass
that would have enabled them to establish significant liberated areas,
which in turn would have engendered more confidence that the
revolution would ultimately succeed and, conversely, created enough
doubts amongst enough people that their support for the Government
might have begun to waver. Nor did the insurgents overall present a
formidable military threat. Seldom, if ever, armed with anything heavier
than a Bren gun – most of which the MPAJA had unwisely handed in
in 1945 – with a critical lack of explosives and demolition experts,
and an almost total lack of radio communication, their scale of
individual operations, although there were perhaps twenty times as
many guerrillas altogether, was comparable to that of Castro and his
comrades in Cuba. The difference in result of course was that, in Malaya
they were faced with a more formidable power than the Batista regime.
Even so, had they had the capacity for destroying armoured cars, the
Malayan insurgents might at least have achieved many more spectacular
successes against the army and police. For communications they were
forced to rely on couriers and paper. Both proved to be their undoing.
The fact that they often kept elaborate records meant that, after a fire
fight when packs of documents were recovered, a great deal of information was revealed. Similarly, when the line of communication was
tapped or cut, one courier or route led back to another and so, eventually, to the guerrilla platoon itself.

In nearly all of these operations the army was eventually kept in its
place and the air force, as an attacking force, was heavily circumscribed.
There were exceptions, but it was operating within the law – admittedly
harsh by today's more relaxed standards – rather than as a law unto
itself. Its place was properly defined as in support of civil power: the
Ulster of today rather than the Ireland of sixty years ago. Its main
function was to provide a framework for counter-guerrilla operations
and when it was realised that troops seldom generate their own intelligence, the police force came into its own in this and other roles, as

the principal arm of civil power. It is in this, its eventual ability to provide information — intelligence — about the pattern of operations and probable location of the guerrillas themselves that one may find the key. It is not a military one. Indeed it is almost the reverse: the assertion that the army, in practice as well as in principle, had to act in support of the civil power which meant that the civil administration was integrated with the police/service effort all the way up — and all the way down.

There was some military 'progress'. Infantry battalions were broken down when it was discovered that they were never needed to fight at that level although, on one or two occasions, that size would have come in handy. Jungle training became more thorough and effective; helicopters were eventually used for troop transport as well as for casualty evacuation. Platoon radio transmitting sets became much more reliable, but in the end the Bren gun, the best weapon when the insurrection began, still weighed just as much when it ended.

Above all, and paradoxically, it may be inferred — although perhaps not consciously intended as such at the time — that the greatest advance was the realisation that regular military units had a fairly subsidiary role. This meant that there was no need for large-scale bombardment, either by artillery or from the air, that, by the greatest of good fortune, there was equally no conceivable excuse for that abominable principle of reconnaissance by fire (if you were in doubt whether a village was 'held' by the enemy you shelled first and inquired later), and that, in practice and very often *faute de mieux*, it was a battle which was fought without a massive superiority in fire power or the remoteness of long-range bombardment. The battles themselves, which can be summed up in two words, 'successful ambush', were only the last and least significant part of a process of more effective government which brought governors and governed into face-to-face and more or less acceptable contact.

Notes

1. Peter Paret and John Shy (eds.), *Guerrillas in the Sixties* (Praeger, New York, 1962), pp. 71–2.

2. Gorden P. Means, *Malaysian Politics* (University of London Press, London, 1970).

3. See e.g. Eric R. Wolf, *Peasant Wars of the Twentieth Century* (Harper & Row, London, 1971), Ch. 6.

4. Charles Gamba, *The Origins of Trade Unions in Malaya* (Eastern Universities Press, Singapore, 1962); M.R. Stenson, *Industrial Conflict in Malaya* (Oxford

University Press, London, 1970); M.R. Stenson, *Repression and Revolt: The Origins of the 1948 Communist Insurrection in Malaya and Singapore* (University of Ohio Press, Athens, 1969) and M.R. Stenson, *The 1948 Communist Revolt in Malaya* (Institute for South-East Asian Studies, Singapore, 1971).

    5. T.R. Gurr, *Why Men Rebel* (Princeton University Press, Princeton, NJ, 1970). Postwar Malayan Chinese might be considered in terms of Gurr's principal characteristic: 'relative deprivation'.

    6. Peter Calvert, *Revolution* (Pall Mall, London, 1970), pp. 112–13.

    7. Spencer Chapman, *The Jungle is Neutral* (Chatto and Windus, London, 1952).

    8. A. Short, 'Nationalism and the Emergency in Malaya' in Michael Leifer (ed.), *Nationalism, Revolution and Evolution in South-East Asia*, (Hull Monographs on South-East Asia, no. 2, 1970), pp. 43–58.

5 THE FRENCH ARMY AND THE ALGERIAN WAR, 1954--62

Alistair Horne

In dealing with the events in Algeria of 1954 to 1962, there is one problem of straightforward English semantics: just as Americans and British differ when they begin to discuss 1776, what the French call 'The Algerian War', the Algerians know simply as 'The Revolution'. It will be referred to here as 'The Algerian War', for simplicity's sake. One further complexity is that during this war (which lasted almost twice as long as the First World War) there were in fact at least seven separate wars, revolutions or struggles, going on upon different planes at the same time. There were, for instance:

(1) The fighting war itself
(2) The political war for the 'middle-ground' in Algeria
(3) A civil war between Algerians
(4) A revolutionary struggle within the leadership of the Algerian FLN: *Front de Libération Nationale*
(5) A struggle between the French Army in Algeria and the Government in Paris, leading in the first place to the overthrow of the Fourth Republic and the advent of de Gaulle, and later to a full-scale revolt against de Gaulle himself
(6) A struggle between the *Pied Noir* settlers of Algeria and France, culminating in open warfare under the aegis of the OAS: *Organisation Armée Secrète*

and finally, and perhaps most decisive:

(7) The external war fought on the platforms of the outside world.

It is the first of these — the fighting war in its military aspects — that will be dealt with here; although, of course, it is impossible to consider it in isolation from the other six. This paper will start by tracing the main chronological events of the war; then go back to sketching out more fully various of the more important factors of particular military interest; and end by putting forward an analysis of some of the lessons left by the Algerian experience.

The French involvement in Algeria goes back to 1830, when landings were carried out near Algiers based closely on plans drawn up by

Napoleon a generation earlier. (These were not deviated from very substantially by the Allied landings in 1942.) The motives for the occupation
were partly a settlement of commercial debts, partly a redress of
national frustration left over from the collapse of the Napoleonic
Empire, but also largely that age-old panacea – to provide a distraction
from discontent at home by pursuit of glory abroad. (Needless to say,
the reigning monarch, Charles X, fell anyway.) Pacification and colonis-
ation absorbed much of French energies for the next half-century. In
1848, the Second Republic took the historical and fateful step of
declaring this vast territory an integral part of France. This made it
unique among all French overseas territories (and, for that matter,
unique among those of any other colonial power); and thus every
government from 1954 onwards, from Mendès-France to de Gaulle, was
lumbered with the albatross round its neck of Algeria being not a colony
but an inseparable part of France herself – like Languedoc or the
Dordogne.

In both World Wars, Algerian *tirailleurs* fought with great bravery,
and loyalty, alongside French metropolitan troops. Then in 1945, no
sooner had Japan capitulated, than a war-weary and economically
rickety France found herself plunged into a *sale guerre* to protect her
empire in Indo-China. Between 1939 and 1962, France was to enjoy
no more than a few weeks of true peace. In May 1954, she lost the
decisive military battle of the Indo-China War at Dien-Bien-Phu.
Prime Minister Mendès-France had barely extricated the country from
Indo-China, when on 1 November 1954 a handful of Algerians (some
of whom had served and seen France humiliated at Dien-Bien-Phu)
launched a revolt across the breadth of Algeria. Armed with almost
visibly slender means, these courageous rebel nationalists called themselves *Front de Libération Nationale.*

The numerous contributory causes of the FLN revolt can only be
dealt with in outline here, but they will not be altogether unfamiliar to
anyone who has studied more contemporary events in Southern Africa:
predominantly, a minority of approximately one million Europeans,
nicknamed *Pieds Noirs* – perhaps because metropolitan Frenchmen
scornfully considered their feet to have been burned black by too much
sun – who were surrounded by a sea of nine million Moslem indigenous
Algerians. Demographically, the Algerian birthrate was exploding;
economically, the gulf between Algerian and *Pied Noir* expectations
was widening, despite considerable French infusions of industry,
capital and know-how. Politically, the Algerians had little more real
power than the Rhodesian blacks under Ian Smith; reforms initiated by

Paris had been the old story of too-little-too-late, and usually torpedoed by the powerful, and conservative, *Pied Noir* lobby. On the other hand, when the revolt began it was supported by only a minority of Algerians.

The French reaction to the revolt, from extreme left to extreme right, was typified by Premier Mendès-France who, though he had got France out of Indo-China, declared of Algeria: 'Ici, c'est la France!' His Minister of the Interior, a good Socialist called Francois Mitterand, took an even more hawkish line: 'the only possible declaration is war . . . for Algeria *is* France . . . '[1] Thus henceforth every French government had its hands tied. Successive Governors-General, like Jacques Soustelle and Robert Lacoste, tried to introduce reforms; vast sums were spent on creating new jobs and housing; but, ahead of reform, each succeeding French Government set as its number one priority first to win the fighting war. Meanwhile, for the Algerians, none of these grandiose reform programmes could quite compete with the magic amulet of *freedom* and *total independence* which the FLN offered from the first in their statement of principles — principles to which they were to adhere with quite remarkable fidelity and rigidity right the way through to 1962.

In the first two years, the war looked unwinnable by either side. The FLN had inadequate equipment to fight more than a series of guerrilla actions, devoting more energy to killing Moslem dignitaries and village policemen and terrorising the non-committed Algerians into joining their side, than to confrontations with the French Army. On the other hand, this huge rugged country of savage mountains, forests and deserts, honeycombed with ravines and caves, provided the ideal territory for fighting a technically superior, modern NATO-style army. The French had not enough troops to be everywhere in this vast territory, now the world's tenth largest nation in area. So in 1956 that other good French Socialist, Guy Mollet, took the dramatic step of first sending half a million conscripts and recalled reservists to Algeria. The most notable effect this had was to spread awareness about the war to Metropolitan France; much as the escalation of the USA's commitment in Vietnam did in America.

Meanwhile the FLN, with consummate skill in canvassing support within the Afro-Asian 'Third World', in the USA and in the United Nations, had gone far to internationalise what France determinedly maintained was a private, internal dispute. In the Autumn of 1956, also under Guy Mollet, the disastrous Suez operation took place. If Britain did not quite know what her aims at Suez were, Mollet certainly did; it was to crush the Algerian revolt by toppling Nasser — whom the

French (exaggeratedly) conceived to be its principal external prop. Almost simultaneously, by a daring *coup-de-main* in mid-air, of somewhat dubious legality, French intelligence hijacked Ben Bella and the entire external leadership of the FLN. But if the abortion of the first episode served only to weaken France's hand in Algeria, the second concentrated the world's gaze still more fixedly on the war, while the presence of Ben Bella and his five fellow prisoners was to prove a constant embarrassment to French policy over the next five-and-a-half years.

In 1957, through resorting to the toughest measures (about which more will be said later) General Massu's elite paras won what looked for the first time like a clear-cut military victory in the famous 'Battle of Algiers'. By the end of the year Massu's forces had captured Yacef, the rebel leader in Algiers, broken up his whole network and severely disrupted the FLN command as a whole.

Meanwhile, on the political level, plane (2), that great *Pied Noir* writer, Albert Camus, had tried in vain to achieve a 'civil truce', but violence escalating into more violence only seemed to ensure the triumph of extremism on either side — with the steady erosion of the Third Force moderates who might one day have formed an anchor for a compromise peace settlement — a depressingly familiar pattern of our times.

In Metropolitan France, the country was reeling from one political crisis to another economic crisis. Governments came and went with dismal regularity, incapable of exerting any influence over events. Everybody was by now fed up with this 'absurd ballet' as de Gaulle scathingly dubbed the gyrations of the Fourth Republic. In April 1958, Premier Gaillard fell, leaving France without a government in the most dangerous power vacuum since 1945. The Algerian War had already toppled five governments, and was about to bring down the Fourth Republic itself. In May the FLN executed three French soldiers; this was the last straw for the hard-tried French Army in Algeria. As de Gaulle says of it:

> Taking upon itself not only the burden of the fighting, but also the severity, and sometimes the beastliness, of the repression, . . . haunted by fear of another Indo-China . . . the army, more than any other body, felt a growing resentment against a political system which was the embodiment of irresolution.[2]

On 13 May, after emotional scenes in Algiers during which *Pied Noir*

ultras, led by an ex-paratrooper called Pierre Lagaillarde, seized and
sacked the Government-General building in Algiers, an army-controlled
'Committee of Public Safety' took over there, under the leadership of
the Commander in Chief, General Raoul Salan. After weeks of con-
spiracy and counter-conspiracy, and a great deal of astute 'playing hard
to get', plus a threat by the paras to drop on France from Algiers (a
scenario alarmingly reminiscent of how Franco detonated the Spanish
Civil War), de Gaulle came off his high perch and, at the ripe age of 67,
agreed to form a government – but on his terms. The Fifth Republic,
and the Gaullist era had begun.

De Gaulle's advent, when he came to Algeria and declared *'je vous
ai compris'* (in fact meaning something far less complimentary to the
Pieds Noirs than they would wish to interpret!), was greeted with
wildest euphoria, by Moslems as well as Europeans. All assumed that
his magic presence would somehow bring peace. But it soon became
tragically apparent that, beneath all the grandiloquence, de Gaulle had
no more of an instant solution to the Algerian War than any of his pre-
decessors. As he busied himself in purging the Augean Stables in France,
crucial months were allowed to pass while he visibly proceeded to do
nothing about Algeria. Much priceless impetus with the Moslem community was sadly allowed to be squandered. Then in October 1958 he
offered the FLN a magnanimously phrased truce offer of a 'Peace of the
Brave'.[3] But it showed the soldier's fundamental miscomprehension of
the political and revolutionary nature of the revolt. Consequently, the
FLN leadership rejected de Gaulle's overture in the most rebuffing terms,
and riposted with the establishment of their first Provisional
Government, the *Gouvernement Provisoire de la République
Algérienne* (GPRA).

The 'Third Force' Moslems who had so rapturously greeted de
Gaulle's advent now increasingly regarded this rebuff as a fatal sign of
weakness. The *Pied Noir* 'ultras', like Lagaillarde, were no less dis-
illusioned. The Army began to distrust de Gaulle, as speaking with too
many different voices; one French observer in 1960 said he was like
Molière's Don Juan who had 'promised marriage to five or six women
and absolutely had to avoid being pinned down by any of them!'[4]
But, in de Gaulle's defence, he felt he could never quite reveal the
whole truth of what he planned to his beloved army, because if he did,
it might revolt and replace him with a military junta, destroying all
his works, as easily as it felt it had brought him to power. This was to
be the source of one of the greatest tragedies in de Gaulle's long career.

Whereas to the French Army and the *Pieds Noirs* Algeria was everything, to de Gaulle it was only one factor in his overall ambition: the resurrection of the greater glory of France – and it was on no account to get in the way of that. On 16 September 1959, he made a key-note speech, offering the Algerians, in those fateful words, 'self-determination'. What he seems to have hoped for was that, through a referendum, they would opt for some kind of limited autonomy in 'association' with France. But to the Army and the *Pied Noirs* it spelled the end of Algérie Française – and this was betrayal. More than ever before the Army was convinced that, under the brilliant General Challe, it was winning the war militarily; less than ever could it see that, in the world outside Algeria, it was being lost politically and diplomatically. In January 1960, the sixth year of the war, the loyal but bombastic General Massu remarked casually to a German journalist that the Army might have made a mistake in bringing back de Gaulle. In a cold rage, de Gaulle sacked Massu. The 'Ultras' had been waiting for just such a detonator, and Algiers exploded. Lagaillarde and a rabble-rousing restaurateur called Jo Ortiz set up an armed and barricaded camp in the centre of the city. When the wretched gendarmes were sent in to move them on, they were met with a withering hail of fire, killing 14 and wounding 123. A grim landmark had been reached; for the first time; Frenchmen were killing Frenchmen. Worst still, some of the elite para units showed every sign of fraternising with the 'Ultras' behind the barricades. Once again, it looked as if France might be facing civil war. Then de Gaulle made one of the greatest speeches of his life; the barricades melted away. But after the irremediable splits that 'Barricades Week' had revealed in the French camp, it was clear to him if to no one else that he had to negotiate. In June 1960, for the first time, the FLN came to the negotiating table, at Melun; but the talks ended in a frosty impasse. De Gaulle had gained nothing, while the FLN 'hardliners' – now headed by the future President, Boumedienne, had won a great moral victory by proving to the world that France was ready to talk. They now applied further pressure on de Gaulle by flirting with Russia and China for military aid.

In December 1960, de Gaulle visited a riot-torn Algeria, in wretched contrast to the euphoric days of two-and-a-half years previously. He narrowly escaped an assassination attempt by a *Pied Noir*. In a powerful backlash, the Moslems appeared on the streets brandishing for the first time in public the green and white banners of the FLN, in their hundreds of thousands, in a turnout that surprised even the FLN. Then, on 21 April, under four senior generals, the Army of Algeria raised a standard of revolt and seized power in Algiers. One of the rebel generals was Salan, the former Commander in Chief who had first opened the door to de Gaulle in May 1958, but of far weightier significance was the leader of the 'Generals' Putsch' — Maurice Challe.

Challe was one of the most esteemed and honourable officers in the French Army — or, for that matter, any army. He had come closer than any other Commander in Chief to winning the war on the ground; but in so doing he had — in the name of de Gaulle — given undertakings to the *Harkis*, or loyal Muslim levies, that France would never abandon them. Chief among his other motives for revolt, Challe felt that the *Harkis* had been traduced (and indeed, in the 'night of long knives' that followed the war their fate was to be a particularly atrocious one) and that honour left him no alternative. Poorly prepared, the revolt lasted four days; but during that time France edged closer to the brink of Civil War than ever before. Ancient tanks tottered out onto the Concorde, and momentarily Parisians expected to see the paras fluttering down from the skies. But once again a superbly timed broadcast by de Gaulle won the day. In the mass, the servicemen and conscripts heeded de Gaulle, rather than their rebel officers, in what became known as the 'Battle of the Transistors'.

However, in spite of De Gaulle's speech, the French Army, 'his army', was badly split — the effects of which can still be seen today. Many of its finest officers had their careers ruined. Challe, expecting the death sentence, spent many years in prison. His was a personal tragedy that should perhaps be pondered by the leaders of other modern democratic armies should they ever come to impose too great a burden upon the conscience of their generals. As for Salan, he went underground as titular leader of the *Organisation Armée Secrète* which, for the remaining months of the war waged a murderous and desperate rearguard action — no longer in the now hopeless cause of Algérie Française, but in the wild hope of somehow creating a *Pied Noir* dominated Algeria, independent of the mother country. When that hope vanished, they launched a campaign of scorched-earth destruction.

With his bargaining hand gravely weakened by the army revolt, and the need to end the war exacerbated by the mounting atrocities of the OAS, de Gaulle now started to negotiate from a position of total weakness; and with what some considered almost indecent haste. Like the peeling of an onion, de Gaulle was forced to abandon the terms he had once hoped to impose one by one; first of all any notion of 'association' with France, then his refusal to negotiate solely with the FLN — thus jettisoning the last surviving Algerian 'moderates'.

Next went the Sahara and its oil. Finally he renounced any valid guarantees for the future of the *Pieds Noirs*.

By its extraordinary, rigid consistency the FLN had won every point it had demanded right back at the beginning of the revolt, leaving de Gaulle shorn even of honour. On 18 March 1962, a ceasefire was signed. By July most of the one million *Pieds Noirs*, in scenes of unparalleled heartbreak, had left behind the homes in which between them, the OAS and the FLN made it impossible for them to remain, in a mass exodus for France or Spain. On 4 July 1962, the tri-colour was lowered in Algiers for the first time in 132 years, curiously enough to the strains of a victory march. The last French High Commissioner, Christian Fouchet, later explained that the music was indeed symbolic for it represented a great victory of the French over themselves. Not everybody would agree with that magnanimous construction. There are undoubtedly those, like former Governor-General Jacques Soustelle, who still consider the French withdrawal from Algeria to have been one of the greatest post-war defeats for the West — along with Dien-Bien-Phu and the USA's abandonment of South Vietnam.

Next, certain specifically military aspects of the war will be examined in greater detail. First, and perhaps most important of all, there is the nature of the French Army itself. The army that fought in Algeria was fundamentally different in character to either the US Army in Vietnam, or the British in Malaya, Kenya, or Cyprus, and this placed its own very particular stamp on the whole of the war — and, indeed, nearly the whole future of France. It was *Le Monde* which once remarked that few armies in the world possess a generation of officers who have fought so much. The names of the Colonels and Generals in Algeria read like a roll of honour of French arms from the post-1940 resurgence onwards. It might also have been added that few modern armies had suffered such a series of dreadfully humiliating defeats; from Sedan in 1940, to Dien-Bien-Phu in 1954, and later Suez in 1956 — all of which, not entirely without reason, the army ascribed more to the deviousness and incompetence of politicians than to any martial failings on its part. The units arriving in Algeria from Indo-China — notably the legendary paras — were well-versed in revolutionary warfare and represented perhaps the toughest and most efficient fighting force in the world at that date. Victories like the 'Battle of Algiers' convinced them that they *could* win the war — and, for deep psychological reasons based on those defeats of the past, it was a war they *had* to win.[5] These tough regulars were, above all, men with a mission:

We want to halt the decadence of the West and the march of
Communism. That is our duty, the real duty of the army. That is
why we must win the war in Algeria. Indo-China taught us to see
the truth,[6]

said Colonel Argoud, an old Indo-China hand who later typified the
ringleaders in the 'Generals' Putsch' against de Gaulle in 1961, and later
still was one of the Fallen Angels of the OAS. But, once again, as the
Argouds and Godards and Salans saw it, the politicians would not let
them win the war.

When the Algerian revolt broke out in November 1954, the French
forces present could hardly have been worse equipped to combat it.
They were a largely mechanised, road-bound force. As a French
ethnologist remarked to an armoured colonel at the time: 'If in 1830
the French Expeditionary Force had had tanks, they wouldn't have got
beyond the beach at Sidi-Ferruch!'[7] There were no mules or horses
available, and only one solitary helicopter in all Algeria. An FLN ambush would surprise a mechanised patrol, burn a vehicle or two, and
kill several men; then melt into the trackless hills. Rebel intelligence
always seemed to be one leap ahead of the cumbersome, weary
French columns. Then the first paras arrived, followed by still more
paras, men like the 'lizards' of the legendary Colonel, later General,
Bigeard. The paras had the advantage of being able to move at
extreme speed, into country that was hitherto almost inaccessible
territory held firmly by the FLN. For a time they turned the tables.
But there were never enough of them to hold ground from which
they had cleared the FLN. So, as in Vietnam, the FLN would return
at night and reterrorise the local *Pied Noir* – or more especially
Moslem farmers.

One of the next developments on the side of the French military
was to introduce the principle of 'collective responsibility', whereby
when telegraph poles were felled or a local dignitary murdered, the
whole Arab community would be held responsible. This had slightly
unpleasant overtones from the Nazi occupation of France and, for
whatever small successes it may have produced, it deeply offended
primitive senses of justice and – in the opinion of more than one
observer – handed the FLN one of its principal 'psychological trump
cards'. Next General Beaufre, perhaps the most thinking general of his
generation, gained temporary success by dividing his command into
three different kinds of zones, which (in a manner similar to that
adopted by the US in Vietnam later) provided for varying degrees of

interdiction, culminating in the *zones interdites* where the army was permitted to fire on anything that moved. This effectively denied the FLN forces access to food and supplies, but it also involved the French authorities in massive resettlement programmes of the peasants living inside the *zones interdites*. These, altogether numbering over a million, were moved into 'Regroupment camps', some of them little better than concentration camps; they were to cause an uproar from French public opinion, and undoubtedly also turned many a previously non-committed Algerian against the French. To this extent the French military defeated their own purpose.

As noted earlier, the paras came from Indo-China thoroughly steeped in the doctrines of Mao and General Giap, and they put these to good use in the methods of psychological and political warfare they introduced into Algeria. One of their most effective principles was to go for the political brain cells of the FLN, the OPA (*Organisation Politico-Administrative*), rather than simply hack away at its military arms. To combat FLN agitation and propaganda in the field, and to maintain the *présence française* in the boondocks, or the *Bled* as it was known, a system called the SAS, *Sections Administratives Spéciales* was instituted. Each of these was run by a dedicated and extremely brave young army officer, usually a captain, who would live among the rural Algerians as a combined mayor, judge, and welfare officer. Unfortunately there were never enough of the good ones to go around, and they were prime targets for the FLN terrorists. It must be said here of the French army officers in the field that, for all the allegations of brutality, many had the most honourable and altruistic motives towards the Algerians. For instance the controversial General Massu himself adopted two Muslim orphans; his wife did an immense amount of welfare work among the underprivileged; and Radio-Bigeard, the paras' own station, was not being insincere when it declared that they had not come to Algeria to defend colonialism, and that the paras really had nothing in common with the rich *colons* who exploited the Muslims.

It must also be noted, however, that to some extent the psychological warfare experts with their Maoist indoctrination seemed to be fighting the wrong enemy. For, although Ho and Giap and the whole Vietminh setup had been thoroughly steeped in Marxist doctrine from the earliest days, communism never had any influence over the FLN. In fact the French Communist Party often ranged itself on the other side. Furthermore, unlike the flesh and blood state on its own soil which the Vietminh inherited, the FLN was always at the disadvantage of having to build up an apparatus, literally, on sand.

We turn back now to the 'Battle of Algiers', beginning in 1956 and
running throughout 1957 – a most important milestone in the military
war. After finding that they were no match, out in the *Bled*, for the
French Army with its new para formations and techniques, the FLN
command tried to make a full-scale bid for supremacy in the city of
Algiers. It began with a sharp increase of urban terrorism and
a general strike timed to coincide with the tabling of the Algieran
problem in the UN. The French gendarmerie proving quite incapable
of mastering the situation, Governor-General Lacoste summoned in
General Massu and his paras. It was a fateful step; among other things
it meant that the army, especially the paras, would be closely involved
in political matters, from which henceforward they would never quite
divorce themselves. Acting with great speed and ruthlessness, the paras
broke the strike, divided up the city in a system of *quadrillage* (which,
their critics in France noted, also bore some resemblance to
Sicherheitsdienst techniques in wartime Paris), and combed minutely
through the hitherto impenetrable maze of the Casbah. Their brilliant
use of informers and the toughest interrogation methods enabled them
to build up an '*organnigramme*' identifying all the leaders and cells in
Yacef's FLN network in Algiers. One by one these were killed or
captured. By the end of 1957, the FLN had to admit its first big
military defeat of the war.

But the Battle of Algiers could probably only have been won with
resort to institutionalised torture – freely admitted by Massu – on a
large scale. The long-term result of this was that, although it may have
won the battle, it probably lost the war for France through the violent
and persistent reaction it aroused both in the mother country and the
world at large.

Therein lies a grave warning for any country which might be
tempted to employ torture as an instrument of policy; it is always
a dangerously double-edged, self-destructive weapon. One distinguished
French soldier has remarked that whatever torture's purpose, it is unacceptable, inadmissible; it soils the honour of the army and the
country.

Just one inevitable consequence of the French Army's resort to
torture, and equally – on the other side – of the appalling atrocities
carried out by the FLN, was the steady erosion of any third force,
any body of moderates, on either side who might one day have formed
the anchor of a compromise peace settlement. Two other indirect
consequences of the 'Battle of Algiers' need to be mentioned. One is
the politicisation of the para leaders. Following Indo-China, one of

the most prominent French military thinkers, General Chassin, after studying the revolutionary lessons of that war, urged the army — which, ever since the 1930s, had been essentially apolitical — to involve itself to an increasing degree of politics. After the 'Battle of Algiers', the paras became more than ever an elitist corps, and needed very little extra persuasion to take Chassin's advice. This led, in a direct line, to the May 1958 coup which brought in de Gaulle; to the fraternising episodes at the time of 'Barricades Week' in January 1960; and finally to the ultimate disaster of the 'Generals' Putsch' of April 1961, in which the para regiments formed the hard core of dissidence — and after which this proud force was extensively broken up.

Secondly, there is the level of intelligence and special operations — at which, incidentally, the French often excelled during the war, whether it involved the assassination of German arms dealers running weapons to the FLN, or under-cover work inside the country. Experiences with double agents, or *bleus*, gained during the Battle of Algiers led to some of the greatest French successes of the whole war. Realising how riven the FLN command was with mutual distrust and rivalries, the French secret services played on this by the skillful introduction of double agents, traitors and forged material into their ranks. This resulted in a bloody series of Stalin-like purges within the FLN army of the interior, to a point where it was almost paralysed. It also gave rise to the one serious bid for a 'separate peace' by the most important of the six FLN commands or 'Wilayas' fighting inside the country. If consummated, the Si Salah episode — or 'Operation Tilsit', as it was called — might have had far-reaching results for an Algerian settlement, to the benefit of France, but it was vetoed by de Gaulle under circumstances that still retain a certain mystery.

Another factor which certainly proved one of the most successful military innovations by the French of the whole war, was the establishment of the Morice Line along both the Tunisian and Moroccan frontiers (notably the former); a kind of Maginot Line, but which, this time, did what it was supposed to do. One is reminded of how materially aided the British were in Malaya, and also Kenya, in having no 'open frontier' with which to cope. The opposite was the deadly Laos trail down along the frontiers of South Vietnam which played such a decisive role in that war against the Americans. The Morice Line was an electrified, mined belt of barbed wire, backed up with radar and mobile fire-power, which lost the FLN thousands of men who had tried to get through to reinforce and supply their hard-pressed forces inside Algeria. It did effectively cut those off from the exterior.

Meanwhile, in 1959, the brilliant General Challe launched a series of the most effective counter-insurgency offensives against the isolated forces in the interior. Building up a powerful mobile reserve, he would sweep one area, leave it held by local forces to prevent the customary return of the FLN, then move on with devastating speed and power to sweep the next area. The Challe technique had never been used before and, combined with the sealing-off effects of the Morice Line, he undoubtedly came closer to winning the military war than had any other commander; this by the beginning of 1960. (It should, however, perhaps also be mentioned that, in terms of men on the ground, whereas France had lost the war in Indo-China with a ratio of 6:4, at the height of the Challe Offensive they enjoyed a superiority of the order of 16:1.)

The very success of Challe's offensive also, unhappily, helped persuade him to his tragic decision to lead the revolt against de Gaulle in 1961, realising that negotiations with the FLN were in the wind. But what Challe, straightforward soldier that he was, could not see was that although the fighting war was virtually won on the ground, it had also been lost on the diplomatic and political fronts of the outside world; in France itself, where – as during the later stages of the US-Vietnam war – protest had risen to unacceptable levels; at the UN, where France had lost most of her friends; and in the US where Senator J.F. Kennedy had led the drive to support the cause of Algerian independence. Meanwhile, on the other side of the Morice Line, Boumedienne had taken the calculated decision more or less to write off the war inside Algeria, and instead build up his troops within the safe sanctuary of Tunisia and Morocco, progressively armed by new Chinese and now Russian weapons, waiting for the decisive day. (This increasing East Bloc involvement was also a factor pressing de Gaulle towards a settlement.)

Thus, it could be said that although militarily the French seemed to have solved the problem of the 'open frontier', that had not been done politically and diplomatically; they might have succeeded in preventing the war spilling into Algeria, but what they had failed to do was to prevent it spilling outwards – into France, the Third World, the UN and the US.

So what were the lessons of France's Algerian War? There are the obvious parallels with Rhodesia; the old sad story of reforms and compromise with the 'moderates' of the interior that come too little and too late; and of course the 'open frontier' with its eternal menace of foreign aid and unlimited externalisation of the war. There is, regrettably, the pessimistic conclusion that in this wicked world terrorism and extremism pays; the moderates lose. Just keep on being obdurate; don't deviate from your maximum terms, and good, moderate, democrat politicians who have to face an election every four or five years will give you what you want, sooner or later! This is perhaps a dishearteningly cynical view; it is to be hoped that some of the young soldiers of today will come to disprove it. Perhaps one of the lessons of the Algerian War particularly is the need for the military of the West to be taught to *think* politically in all situations, and to be *in touch* politically; but *not* to get *involved* politically. It is a difficult and dangerous tightrope to have to walk.

Notes

1. Alistair Horne, *A Savage War of Peace, Algeria, 1954–1962* (Macmillan, London, 1977), pp. 98–9.
2. Charles de Gaulle, *Memoirs of Hope*, Terrance Kilmartin (trans.) (Weidenfeld and Nicolson, London, 1971), p. 15.
3. Horne, *A Savage War of Peace*, pp. 301–6.
4. Ibid., p. 377.
5. Ibid., pp. 165–7.
6. Colonel Antoine Argoud, November 1960.
7. Horne, *A Savage War of Peace*, p. 100.
8. For an elaboration of the implications and lessons of France's Algerian War see 'The Page is Turned', ibid., Chapter 25, pp. 535–62.

Further Readings

Behr, Edward, *The Algerian Problem* (Hodder and Stoughton, London, 1961)

Clark, Michael K., *Algeria in Turmoil, A History of the Rebellion* (Thames and Hudson, London, 1960)

Courrière, Yves, *La Guerre d'Algérie*, 4 vols. (Fayard, Paris); vol. 1, *Les Fils de la Toussaint* (1960); vol. 2, *Les Temps des Léopard* (1969); vol. 3, *L'heure des Colonels* (1970) and vol. 4, *Les Feur de du déspoir, La Fin d'un Empire* (1971)

Gordon, David C., *The Passing of French Algeria* (Oxford, London, 1966)

Jurridini, P.A. *et al.*, *A Casebook on Insurgency and Revolutionary Warfare: Algeria, 1954–1962* (Special Operations Research Office, Washington, DC, 1963)

Quandt, William B., *Revolution and Political Leadership: Algeria,*

1954–1968 (Massachusetts Institute of Technology Press, Cambridge, 1969) and *Algerian Military Development, Professionalisation of a Guerrilla Army* (Rand Corporation, Santa Monica, California, 1972)

Tricot, Bernard, *Les Sentiers de la Paix, Algérie, 1958–1962* (Librarie Plon, Paris, 1972)

Tripier, Phillipe, *Autopsie de la Guerre d'Algérie* (France-Empire, Paris, 1972)

AMERICA AND VIETNAM: THE FAILURE OF
STRATEGY

Herbert Y. Schandler

Vietnam was a political and military disaster for the United States.
Although the US military forces won every battle, the nation was unable to pursue the war to a satisfactory conclusion. This produced a
rather short-lived national trauma, but the effects have conditioned
American policy in many other areas of the world. Some have concluded that the whole effort was for naught. Indeed, some have
questioned the utility of military force, based upon the Vietnam
experience, as a viable instrument of American foreign policy in the
future.

The causes for this failure, however, have never been carefully
examined nor has corrective action been taken. America's very
reluctance to face up to the reality of its experience there certainly
signals the need for a better understanding of the US effort in
Vietnam.

American failure in Vietnam was both strategic and tactical. In both
cases, political and military objectives were not clear and the strategy
and concept of operations adopted did not accord with the realities of
the situation. American introspection and lack of knowledge, indeed
unwillingness to seek knowledge, of a foreign culture and of the
motivations of a dedicated enemy led to policies which did not address
the actual problem, but addressed only problems that they chose to see.
In response to a new challenge, to an unconventional threat, the US
response was almost entirely conventional. The Americans fought the
war American-style rather than adapting their responses to the nature
of the conflict.

National Strategy and Political Objectives

On the national level, the successful defence of South Vietnam was seen
by Lyndon Johnson to be essential to the domestic political well-being
of the United States. The President felt that the alternative to defending
South Vietnam would not be peace but an expanded area of conflict
and a diminution of American power and credibility elsewhere in the
world. Vietnam itself was not seen as of overwhelming strategic importance to the United States. Rather it was seen as a test of the United
States' military commitments to its allies around the world, as a vital

clash of wills between communism and the system of alliances
established by the United States after World War II. It was the testing
ground where the challenge of communist wars of national liberation
would be met by counter-insurgency warfare. To not intervene and
assist this beleaguered ally, the President felt, meant that communism
would spread throughout South-East Asia; other United States commitments would be called into question and the nation would be split by
a vicious internal debate as to the wisdom of the policy adopted.
President Johnson has been quoted as saying, as early as 1963, 'I am
not going to be the President who saw South-East Asia go the way
China went.'[1]

The long-term goal was a political settlement that would 'allow the
South Vietnamese to determine their own future without outside inter-
ference'. In a speech at Johns Hopkins University in April 1965, the
President laid out for the American people what would be done in
Vietnam: 'We will do everything necessary to reach that objective
[that the people of South Vietnam be allowed to guide their own
country in their own way]. And we will do only what is absolutely
necessary.'[2]

Thus, Johnson's policy objectives translated into doing the minimum
amount militarily to preventing a South Vietnam defeat while convincing
Hanoi that it would not succeed in its aggression.

To the President and his Secretary of Defence, then, this policy
meant a war for limited purposes using limited resources in a
geographically constricted area. The allocation of American manpower
and resources would not be allowed to reach the point where the war
would unduly affect the civilian economy or interfere with the
programmes of the Great Society. Operations would be restricted
geographically so as not to incite Soviet or Chinese intervention.

The objective was not to 'win', either in North or South Vietnam,
but rather to convince the North Vietnamese (and their Soviet and
Chinese sponsors) that the cost of continuing the war in South
Vietnam would be, over time, prohibitive to them and that they could
not succeed. In actuality, however, there was no clear conception as to
when this elusive psychological goal would be achieved. The President's
strategy, then, was defensive in nature and, in effect, left the decision
as to when to end the war in the hands of North Vietnam. And as we
know, this strategy greatly underestimated the willingness of the old
revolutionaries in Hanoi to take terrible punishment in the pursuit of
their objectives in the South.

In addition, this rather simplistic strategy saw the conflict in South

Vietnam as a communist aggression in the cold war model — a challenge
to a free nation by expansionist international communism. The
questionable legitimacy of the South Vietnamese Government, and the
nationalist and anti-colonial motives and credentials of North Vietnam
were overlooked. Thus, the enemy was much too narrowly defined and
the Saigon government was ascribed capabilities which it never possessed.

But the Joint Chiefs of Staff saw this limited political objective as
essentially negative and ineffective. It yielded the initiative to the
enemy and placed primary reliance upon the undependable South
Vietnamese armed forces. The Joint Chiefs felt that a more ambitious
objective was necessary, that of defeating the enemy both in North
and South Vietnam. They advocated the classic doctrine that victory
depended upon the rapid application of overwhelming military power
through offensive action to defeat the enemy's main forces.

The Joint Chiefs saw three equally important military tasks to be
accomplished in Vietnam:

(1) To cause the Democratic Republic of Vietnam (North Vietnam)
    to cease its direction and support of the Viet Cong insurgency;
(2) To defeat the Viet Cong and to extend the Government of
    Vietnam's (GVN) control over all of South Vietnam;
(3) To deter Communist China from direct intervention and to
    defeat such intervention if it should occur.[3]

Thus, in the air war, the military chiefs advocated a forceful bombing
campaign, with steadily increasing pressure against North Vietnam. In
the South, the military chiefs advocated a strategy of taking the war to
the enemy wherever he might appear, attacking his main force elements
in South Vietnam and his sanctuaries and support installations in Laos
and Cambodia. This strategy, of course, would leave US military
commitments to Vietnam virtually open-ended.

This debate concerning the strategy advocated by the President and
his civilian advisors and the more forceful strategy advocated by the
military chiefs continued throughout Lyndon Johnson's presidency.
The Joint Chiefs of Staff continued to request additional American
troops in South Vietnam, increased bombing of North Vietnam, and
expanded operational authority in Laos, Cambodia, and North
Vietnam. They felt that their strategy for 'winning' the war was
thwarted by the availability to enemy troops of sanctuaries and supply
routes in Laos and Cambodia where they could refit, re-equip, and
escape destruction by American ground and air power. Further, the

constraints on the use of air power in North Vietnam, they felt, allowed the enemy to adjust to the bombing campaign so that its pressure did not become unacceptable. Of equal consequence and concern to the military chiefs was the fact that the decision not to call up reserve forces depleted American active forces outside of Vietnam to the point where the nation might not be able to respond to military contingencies elsewhere.

The President and his Secretary of Defence continued to disapprove additional operational authority, however, and approved only that gradual force buildup which could be supported without the necessity for a reserve mobilisation. As the war developed, the debate within the Administration concerning the level of American effort in South Vietnam, in fact, came to devolve around this one crucial issue of mobilisation. When the President searched for the elusive point at which the costs of the effort in Vietnam would become unacceptable to the American people, he always settled upon mobilisation, that point at which reserves would have to be called up to support the war. This domestic constraint, with all its political and social repercussions, not any argument concerning military strategy, appears to have dictated American war policy.

Denied a strategic concept and the military freedom they felt was necessary to win the war, the military chiefs were pacified by gradual increases in force levels and in bombing targets and, eventually, by the replacement of a Secretary of Defence who had become anathema to them. But these increases in military authority and resources were always within the President's guidelines. Lyndon Johnson retained the political constraints upon military actions and, in effect, determined his own strategy, based upon domestic political considerations.

Thus, fundamental differences concerning American objectives in South Vietnam were never resolved nor were these differences brought to the surface publicly. Decisions concerning the allocation of American resources to Vietnam were made on the basis of what was the minimum additional that could be done while maintaining public support for the war. This domestic consideration dictated the minimum necessary disruption in American life. There was no agreed coherent strategy to achieve American objectives and, indeed, no agreement as to those objectives. The President made at least eight separate decisions concerning United States force levels in Vietnam over a four-year period. The issues addressed and the decisions that were made were always tactical in nature. The only alternative policies examined, or decided upon, were alternative force levels or alternative bombing campaigns. On the other hand, the Joint Chiefs of Staff made no independent analyses of what force would be needed to achieve US objectives within the restraints placed upon military operations by the President, nor of what actually could be achieved within those constraints. Their advice was always predictable: 'Do what General Westmoreland asks; lift the political and geographic restraints under which our forces operate, and increase the size of the strategic reserve.'[4]

So the effort at the national level was piecemeal and misdirected. Each decision represented a compromise between a President determined to preserve his domestic programmes while defending freedom in South-East Asia and the Joint Chiefs of Staff who saw no alternative but an American takeover of the war and an all out effort against a dangerous and tenacious enemy, while mobilising to maintain American military capabilities to deal with contingencies in other parts of the world.

The consequences of this failure to develop a precise clear aim with necessary limitations, consequences certainly unintended by President Johnson, were a large-scale bombing campaign against North Vietnam and the commitment of half a million American troops to a ground war in Asia without any fundamental agreement as to how victory was to be achieved.

The Tactical Concept

On the ground in Vietnam — on the tactical level — this disagreement as to the military strategy to be pursued was mirrored. The mission assigned the first American troops to land in Vietnam, in March 1965, was to secure the airbase at Danang and supporting installations and facilities. The orders clearly stated, 'The US Marine Force will not, repeat will not, engage in day to day actions against the Viet Cong.'[5]

The policy of using these forces only for base security was short-lived, however, The Marines hardly had their feet dry when several proposals were brought forward to get US troops actively engaged in the ground war. A change in mission for US ground forces in Vietnam was sanctioned in April, although in very cautious language: 'The President approved a change of mission for all Marine battalions deployed to Vietnam to permit their more active use under conditions to be established and approved by the Secretary of Defense in consultation with the Secretary of State.'[6]

This decision, although it did not clearly define the new mission, was a pivotal one. It marked the President's acceptance of the concept that US troops would engage in offensive ground operations against an

Asian foe. To be sure, the language indicated a desire to proceed slowly and carefully. But missing was any concept of a unified, coherent tactical concept for the use of American ground forces. That issue took the form of a debate between advocates of an enclave defence and those who advocated an all out military struggle of attrition. The enclave concept, first proposed by General Harold K. Johnson in 1965, was tenaciously advocated by Ambassador Taylor. Taylor saw many advantages to it:

> The . . . role which has been suggested for US ground forces is the occupation and defense of key enclaves along the coast such as Quang Ngai, Qui Nhon, Tuy Hoa and Nha Trang. Such a disposition would have the advantage of placing our forces in areas of easy access and egress with minimum logistic problems associated with supply and maintenance. The presence of our troops would assure the defense of these important key areas and would relieve some GVN forces for employment elsewhere. The troops would not be called upon to engage in counter-insurgency operations except in their own local defense and hence would be exposed to minimum losses.[7]

Thus, the enclave strategy envisaged denying the enemy victory because he would be unable to seize decisive areas held by US forces, despite whatever successes he might enjoy throughout the rest of the country. Realising his inability to gain a final victory, the enemy would be moved to a negotiated settlement of the conflict. Also, US forces would be limited in number, could be brought in and supplied with ease over sea lines of communications controlled entirely by the US Navy, and could be withdrawn with equal ease should the situation so dictate. Beyond the enclaves, the South Vietnamese army would be expected to continue to prosecute the war against the enemy's main forces.

But as Ambassador Taylor had also pointed out, the enclave concept was 'a rather inglorious static defensive mission unappealing to them [US forces] and unimpressive in the eyes of the Vietnamese.'[8] It was perceived by the military commanders as a negative defensive concept, yielding the initiative to the enemy and designed to frustrate rather than to defeat him.

On the other side, as General Westmoreland saw it:

> I am convinced that US troops with their energy, mobility, and

firepower can successfully take the fight to the VC. The basic purpose of the additional deployments . . . is to give us a substantial and hard hitting offensive capability on the ground.[9]

In requesting a buildup to a total of thirty-five manoeuvre battalions, with a further nine battalions to be prepared for deployment if needed at a later date, Westmoreland spelled out his concept for employing these forces. Sweeping away the last vestiges of the enclave concept, he described his plans for assuming the offensive and defeating the enemy. He saw the war developing in three distinct phases as follows:

(Phase I) Commitment of US (and other Free World) forces necessary to halt the losing trend by the end of 1965.

(Phase II) US and Allied forces mount major offensive actions to seize the initiative to destroy guerrilla and organised enemy forces. This phase would be concluded when the enemy had been worn down, thrown on the defensive, and driven back from the major populated areas.

(Phase III) If the enemy persisted, a period of a year to a year and a half following Phase II would be required for the final destruction of enemy forces remaining in remote base areas.[10]

There was no mention in General Westmoreland's plan of a political offensive to 'win the hearts and minds of the people'. There was no recognition of the North Vietnamese strategy of people's war. The concept was a traditional military one, that of defeating the enemy's military forces and driving them from the battlefield.

This tactical concept of operations tended to concentrate on the Viet Cong military units in the hope that defeat of these units would cause the insurgency to collapse. This tactic ignored the political strength of the underground organisation and thus failed to deal with a very critical dimension of the problem.

President Johnson, on 28 July 1965, approved the deployment to South Vietnam of General Westmoreland's thirty-five battalion force totalling 175,000 troops (later raised to 219,000).[11] Whatever they may have thought personally of the wisdom of this momentous decision of July 1965, all the participants realised that a major threshold had been crossed. A new course had been taken, the end of which was not in sight. As General Westmoreland understood:

Explicit in my forty-four battalion proposal and President Johnson's approval of it was a proviso for free manoeuver of American and allied units throughout South Vietnam. Thus the restrictive enclave strategy with which I had disagreed from the first was finally rejected.[12]

And as Johnson later stated, 'Now we were committed to major combat in Vietnam.'[13]

Accompanying this change from enclave defence to offensive 'search and destroy' operations, as they came to be called, was a subtle, but extremely significant, change in emphasis. Instead of the limited political objective of simply denying the enemy victory and convincing him that he would not win, the military pursued the chimera of a military victory to be won by defeating the enemy on the ground of South Vietnam. National policy no longer coincided with the objectives being pursued by the field commander. General Westmoreland had explicit directives on what he was not to do, imprecise instructions on what he was expected to accomplish (although he had set his own goals), and very vague information on what forces he would have on hand to accomplish what he thought he wanted to do.

Execution

The force approved by President Johnson in July 1965 was recognised as sufficient only to prevent the collapse of South Vietnam while the stage was being set for further US troop deployments. But the establishment by the military of the goal of defeating the enemy rather than merely denying him victory opened the door to an indeterminate amount of additional force. The amount of forces required to defeat the enemy depended entirely on the enemy's response to the US buildup and his willingness to increase his own commitment to the struggle.

Although US forces could maintain the tactical initiative in South Vietnam through their great mobility and firepower, the enemy maintained the strategic initiative throughout by his willingness to increase his commitment of forces to the struggle. Thus, the pace and level of the fighting would be dictated by the enemy and not by the United States.

From this point on, the American response in Vietnam was a conventional military one. The military defeat of the enemy seemed an achieveable goal, and the US army escalated and re-escalated in order to progress toward that goal. The defeat of the enemy became an end in itself, as it had been in more conventional American wars. But the operational restrictions imposed by the President made the task of defeating the enemy more difficult, even dooming Westmoreland's strategy of attrition to failure.

The Viet Cong and the regular North Vietnamese units were not vulnerable to US ground forces until they crossed the borders into South Vietnam. Likewise, enemy units in South Vietnam could escape pursuit and engagement by US units by crossing over the borders into Cambodia, Laos, or into the Demilitarised Zone (DMZ). Thus the enemy could enter the battle when he wished and could withdraw from the battlefield when he chose. This made attrition very difficult.

Success in the war of attrition did not depend on General Westmoreland's ability to defeat the enemy in the field; it depended instead on how long the North Vietnamese were willing to feed the pipeline with men, equipment and supplies. The strategy granted advantages to the enemy that could not be overcome by US actions in the field. If the enemy was willing to pay the price, he could keep the US army tied up indefinitely. And as it turned out, he was willing to pay a very high price.

Likewise, to the extent that American concentration on military forces in the field led to neglect of the underground organisation, the strategy of attrition was misdirected. There was little or no realisation of the revolutionary dynamics of the situation, the popular appeal of the Viet Cong, or the weakness of the half-formed, traditionalist military regimes in Saigon. There was little realisation that critical to security was the development of an honest and efficient South Vietnamese government committed to administering justice and to improving the welfare of its people.

In fact, the acceptance of the buildup of US forces and their use in an offensive role throughout Vietnam was an explicit expression of a total loss of confidence in the South Vietnamese Armed Forces (RVNAF) and a concomitant willingness on the part of US commanders to take over the major part of the war effort. The paradox arose of the Americans fighting on behalf of an army (and a government) that they treated with disdain, even contempt. The South Vietnamese, on whose behalf the United States had entered a land war in Asia, were dealt with as if they really weren't worth saving. Thus, there grew a naked contradiction between the political objectives of the war and the actual situation of virtually ignoring the South Vietnamese government and army in the formulation of American strategy.

Military operations were seldom coordinated with or directed toward progress in the pacification programme. Military leaders on the ground failed to grasp the causes or the significance of the steady attrition of

GVN authority in the countryside, a loss of political authority that was directly linked to the way the war was conducted. Indeed, the effects of military operations – the uprooting of the rural populace, its concentration in refugee camps or in the large cities of South Vietnam, the creation of 'free fire zones', the breakdown of government in the rural areas, the demoralisation of many aspects of traditional Vietnamese life – worked against the pacification programme. As one observer noted:

> Instead of the weaknesses within South Vietnam being eliminated they were being aggravated . . . It was never understood that nation building was the offensive construction programme designed to strengthen the government's assets and eliminate its weaknesses, while the military operations were defensive and destructive, designed to hold the ring for the constructive programme and, in so doing, to weaken the enemy's military assets.[14]

So the many and spectacular American military victories over Viet Cong/North Vietnamese Army forces could not be translated into political gains for the South Vietnamese government. When American forces withdrew from an area, the enemy continued to find shelter, or at least passive acquiescence to his presence, from the rural population of South Vietnam. The two wars, political and military, were pursued as two relatively unrelated activities. But success in the military war could make no lasting difference without corresponding success in the political war.

There was some recognition that more was needed in Vietnam. Lip service was given to a 'positive programme', to 'pacification' or 'revolutionary development' programmes designed to bring social justice to the countryside in order to win the 'hearts and minds' of the people and gain their active support for a government interested in their welfare and responsive to their needs. But comparatively meagre resources were devoted to this programme, and they were devoted too late. Often, such programmes as were developed were largely planned, financed and implemented by Americans with little GVN involvement. And again, there was no agency within the United States government solely responsible for such programmes. The State Department certainly abnegated such a role and, after the introduction of large numbers of American forces, the US embassy in Saigon limited its roles to the traditional ones of representation and reporting on, rather than trying to influence, political developments.

Thus, the administration of American civil programmes in Vietnam was marked by fragmented and inefficient planning and execution. An innovative and unique organisation which integrated all US civil and military pacification support and provided a single channel of advice and assistance to the Vietnamese at all levels was finally instituted in Vietnam, under the overall direction of General Westmoreland, and not the Ambassador, in May 1967. Unfortunately, unification in the field was not paralleled by similar unification among the many interested agencies in Washington, and these programmes remained superficial and achieved few lasting results. Indeed, there was a general shallowness of knowledge and indifference to consideration of South Vietnam as a society with its own structures and history. Even though a constitution was written and democratic elections were held at the national level, the basic structure of South Vietnamese society, government, and power relationships was not disturbed. And so the existence of South Vietnam as a nation continued to be sustained, as it had been at the outset of the American involvement, only by the commitment of American military power.

Analysis

Political science provides no clear prescription for the development of a viable democratic political system in a traditional society recently freed from colonial rule, with limited physical and administrative resources, and in the midst of a bitter civil war. Certainly, there is no agency of the United States government charged with such a task. Therefore, there must be some doubt as to what could have been accomplished along such lines by an outside power in an alien society even if a clear realisation of the true problem had been present. But this dimension of the problem was never addressed. The American response was a conventional military response alone.

The American failure in Vietnam up to the time of Tet was not a failure caused by the limitations placed upon military action, as some military leaders and other commentators continue to charge.[15] Indeed, overwhelming American military power was brought to bear. The United States enjoyed complete control of the sea and air and had a striking superiority in men and equipment on land. The American failure was caused by the lack of realisation that military power alone could not solve what was basically a political problem. Overwhelming American military power was never directed toward solving that political problem. Military power was never used in ways that would contribute to the political stability and competence of the Saigon government. As one participant has stated: 'In the last analysis, the US effort in Vietnam — at least through 1967 — failed largely because it could not sufficiently revamp or adequately substitute for a South Vietnamese leadership, administration, and armed forces inadequate to the task.'[16]

As former Secretary of State Henry Kissinger has written, perhaps this lesson has now been learnt, but it has been learnt too late:

> We have learned important lessons from the tragedy of Indochina — most importantly that outside effort can only supplement, but not create, local efforts and local will to resist... And there is no question that popular will and social justice are, in the last analysis, the essential underpinning of resistance to subversion and external challenge.[17]

Notes

1. Tom Wicker, *JFK and LBJ: The Influence of Personality on Politics* (Morrow, New York, 1968), p. 208.
2. *Public Papers of the Presidents: Lyndon B. Johnson, 1965*, vol. 1 (US Government Printing Office, Washington, 1966), p. 395.
3. JCSM 652-65, 27 August 1965, Subject: *Concept for Vietnam*, quoted in *US-Vietnam Relations, 1945–1967* (US Government Printing Office, Washington, 1971), IV C(6) (a), p. 74.
4. Alain C. Enthoven and Wayne K. Smith, *How Much is Enough? Shaping the Defense Programme, 1961–1969* (Harper and Row, New York, 1971), pp. 299–300.
5. *US-Vietnam Relations, 1945–1967*, IV C(4) (a), p. 1.
6. Ibid., IV C(5), pp. 68–9, 124–6; Lyndon B. Johnson, *The Vantage Point: Perspectives of the Presidency, 1963–1969* (Holt, Rinehart and Winston, New York, 1971), pp. 140–1.
7. *US-Vietnam Relations, 1945–1967*, IV C(3), p. 57.
8. Ibid., p. 58; General William C. Westmoreland, *A Soldier Reports* (Doubleday and Co., Garden City, 1976), pp. 129–30.
9. Military Assistance Command Vietnam 19118, 070335Z, June 1965, MACV to Commander in Chief United States Forces Pacific.
10. General William C. Westmoreland, *Report on the War in Vietnam: Section II, Report on Operations in South Vietnam, January 1964–June 1968* (US Government Printing Office, Washington, 1969), p. 100; *US-Vietnam Relations, 1945–1967*, IV C(5), pp. 118–19.
11. *Public Papers of the President: Lyndon B. Johnson, 1965*, vol. II, pp. 794–9.
12. Westmoreland, *A Soldier Reports*, pp. 144, 146–52.
13. Johnson, *The Vantage Point: Perspectives of the Presidency, 1963–1969*, p. 153.
14. Sir Robert G.K. Thompson, *No Exit From Vietnam* (Chatto and Windus, London, 1969), pp. 146, 149.
15. Westmoreland, *A Soldier Reports*, pp. 410–11; Drew Middleton, *Can*

America Win the Next War? (Charles Scribners' Sons, New York, 1975), pp. 5–6.

16. R.W. Komer, *Bureaucracy Does Its Thing: Institutional Constratins on US – GVN Performance in Vietnam* (The Rand Corporation, Santa Monica, 1972), p. 18.

17. *Department of State Bulletin*, vol. 73, US Department of State, pp. 3–4.

NOTES ON CONTRIBUTORS

Ronald Haycock is Assistant Professor of History at the Royal Military College of Canada. Born in Ingersoll, Ontario, Dr Haycock received his education at Waterloo Lutheran University, the University of Waterloo and the University of Western Ontario. He is author of the *Image of the Indian* (1971) and in 1978 was the Symposium Director for RMC's Fifth Annual Military History Symposium on 'Regular Armies and Insurgency'.

Alistair Alan Horne, FRSL, is an historian, journalist and lecturer. He received his MA at Cambridge. Mr Horne served in the RAF, the Coldstream Guards and with the British Intelligence Service from 1939–47. As an historian, he has published widely. Among his books are *Canada and the Canadians* (1961); *The Price of Glory: Verdun 1916* (for which he received the Hawthornden Prize in 1962); *To Lose a Battle: France 1940* (1969); *Death of a Generation* (1970); and *The Paris Commune, 1871* (1971). His latest work, a history of the French Army in the Algerian War, *A Savage War of Peace* appeared in 1977 and was given the Wolfson Literary Award for History in 1978.

Dr Edwin Lieuwen is Professor of Latin American History at the University of New Mexico. Dr Lieuwen has also taught at the University of California, Los Angeles, and Berkeley. He has received Fulbright, Carnegie and Rockefeller Foundation awards, and has been a political advisor on Latin America to the Government of the United States. For ten years he served as Chairman of the History Department at the University of New Mexico. He has published several books on Latin American politics and militarism, some of which are *Arms and Politics in Latin America* (1964), *Generals versus Presidents: Neo-militarism in Latin America* (1965), and *Militarism in Mexico* (1968). He is currently writing a biography of the Mexican Revolutionary, General Alvaro Obregón.

Colonel Herbert Y. Schandler, PhD, US Army (retired). Colonel Schandler was for 23 years a professional soldier, having graduated from West Point in 1952. He served in Korea, as a Green Beret Commander in Germany and as an infantry battalion commander in

Vietnam. He was also a special advisor to General Westmoreland on pacification programmes in Vietnam and a specialist in Vietnam and South-East Asian affairs for the US government. In 1966, he was assigned to the Revolutionary Development Division, US Military Assistance Command, Saigon. He participated in the planning for the Paris peace talks on Vietnam, and contributed substantially to the Pentagon Papers. Dr Schandler received his PhD from Harvard in 1974 and has taught at West Point and the University of Maryland. In 1977 he published *The Unmaking of a President: Lyndon Johnson and Vietnam*, while acting as the specialist in National Defence, Congressional Research Service at the Library of Congress.

Anthony Short was born in Singapore and did his military service in Malaya. He was with his battalion when the insurrection began and subsequently served in Johore. Educated at the Universities of Exeter, London, Virginia and Oxford, he taught for six years in the History Department of the University of Malaya. Shortly after his arrival there, he was approached by the Government of Malaya to write, without censorship and with full access to secret documents, the history of the communist insurrection. However, when he presented this manuscript, he was told by the Malayan Government that for reasons of national security it would not be published. Despite these impediments, Dr Short succeeded in having it published in Great Britain as *The Communist Insurrection in Malaya, 1948–1960*. He is now Senior Lecturer in Politics and Warden of Dunbar Hall at Aberdeen University.

Sir Robert G.K. Thompson, KBE, CMG, DSO, MC, is formerly of the Malayan Civil Service which he joined in 1938. After a distinguished career in the RAF in the Far East during the Second World War, he held a variety of posts in Malaya. Among these positions were those involved in the defence of the country during the Emergency. In 1961 Sir Robert was appointed head of the British Advisory Mission to Vietnam. He has also served as a consultant to various governments including the United States. He is recognised as an authority on counter-insurgency warfare and has written and lectured widely on the subject. His major publications are *Defeating Communist Insurgency* (1966); *No Exit from Vietnam* (1969); *Revolutionary War in World Strategy 1945–1969* (1970); and *Peace is Not at Hand* (1974).

Charles Townshend received his BA and DPhil from Oxford University. Among his publications, *The British Campaign in Ireland, 1919–1921* was considered by A.J.P. Taylor to be the best book on history in 1975. Dr Townshend now teaches at the University of Keele.

INDEX